Rick Steves®

POCKET

FLORENCE

Rick Steves & Gene Openshaw

Contents

PHOTO CREDITS

Maximize your travel skills with a good guidebook.

RickSteves.com @RickSteves

Rick Steves books are available at bookstores
and through online booksellers.

Introduction

Florence is Europe's cultural capital. As the home of the Renaissance and birthplace of the modern world, Florence practiced the art of civilized living back when the rest of Europe was rural and crude.

Florence is geographically small, with more artistic masterpieces per square mile than anyplace else. In a single day, you can look Michelangelo's *David* in the eyes, fall under the seductive sway of Botticelli's *Birth of Venus,* and climb the modern world's first dome, which still dominates the skyline.

Today's Florence bustles with a modern vibe coursing through its narrow Renaissance lanes. You'll encounter children licking gelato, students riding Vespas, supermodels wearing Gucci fashions, and artisans sipping Chianti—many of the very things you came to Italy to see.

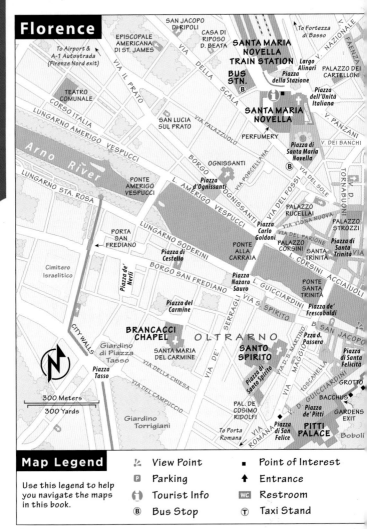

Florence

To Airport &
A-1 Autostrada
(Firenze Nord exit)

SAN JACOPO
DI RIPOLI

CASA DI
RIPOSO
D. BEATA

EPISCOPALE
AMERICANA
DI ST. JAMES

SANTA MARIA
NOVELLA
TRAIN STATION

To Fortezza
di Basso

BUS
STN.

Largo
Alinari

PALAZZO DEI
CARTELLONI

TEATRO
COMUNALE

Piazza
della Stazione

Piazza
dell'Unità
Italiana

SANTA MARIA
NOVELLA

SAN LUCIA
SUL PRATO

PERFUMERY

V. PANZANI

Arno River

OGNISSANTI

Piazza
d'Ognissanti

Piazza di
Santa Maria
Novella

V. DEI BANCHI

PONTE
AMERIGO
VESPUCCI

PORTA SAN
FREDIANO

Piazza di
Cestello

PONTE
ALLA
CARRAIA

Piazza
Carlo
Goldoni

PALAZZO
RUCELLAI

PALAZZO
CORSINI

PALAZZO
STROZZI

Piazza di
Santa
Trinità

Cimitero
Israelitico

Piazza de'
Nerli

BORGO SAN FREDIANO

Piazza
Nazaro
Sauro

SANTA
TRINITÀ

PONTE
SANTA
TRINITÀ

Piazza de'
Frescobaldi

Piazza del
Carmine

BRANCACCI
CHAPEL

OLTRARNO

SANTO
SPIRITO

B. SAN JACOPO

Piazza di
Santa
Felicità

Giardino
di Piazza
Tasso

SANTA MARIA
DEL CARMINE

Pzza d.
Passera

Piazza
Tasso

Piazza di
Santo Spirito

GROTTO

BACCHUS

300 Meters

300 Yards

PAL. DE
COSIMO
RIDOLFI

Piazza
de' Pitti

GARDENS
EXIT

Giardino
Torrigiani

To Porta
Romana

Piazza
di San
Felice

PITTI
PALACE

Boboli

Map Legend

Use this legend to help
you navigate the maps
in this book.

View Point

Point of Interest

Parking

Entrance

Tourist Info

WC Restroom

Bus Stop

Taxi Stand

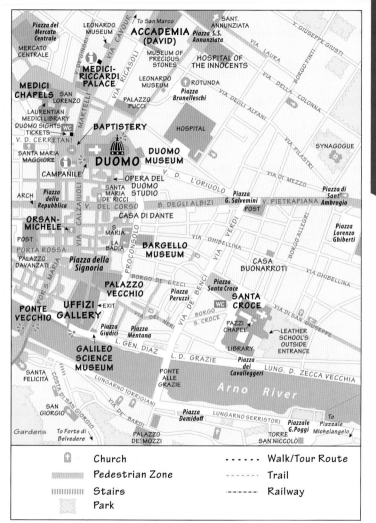

⌂	Church
▨	Pedestrian Zone
⫼	Stairs
▦	Park

······	Walk/Tour Route
------	Trail
━━━	Railway

About This Book

With this book, I've selected only the best of Florence—admittedly, a tough call. The core of the book is five self-guided tours that zero in on Florence's greatest sights and neighborhoods.

My Renaissance Walk leads you through the historic core—a great introduction to the town's layout, history, and major sights. The Accademia/*David* Tour stars Michelangelo's 17-foot-tall colossus... 'nuff said? The Uffizi Gallery Tour presents the world's greatest collection of Italian painting. And at the Bargello and Duomo museums, you'll see some of the world's best sculpture.

The rest of the book is a traveler's tool kit. You'll find plenty more about Florence's attractions, from shopping to nightlife to less touristy sights. And there are helpful hints on saving money, avoiding crowds, getting around town, enjoying a great meal, and more.

Florence by Neighborhood

The best of Florence (population 380,000) lies on the north bank of the Arno River. The main historical sights cluster around the red-brick dome of the cathedral (Duomo). Everything is within a 20-minute walk of the cathedral, train station, or Ponte Vecchio (Old Bridge). Much of this historic core is now delightfully traffic-free. For easy orientation, think of Florence divided into sections:

The Duomo to the Arno: The historic spine stretches from the cathedral to the Palazzo Vecchio (with its tall medieval spire) to the Uffizi Gallery to the Ponte Vecchio. It's an easy 10-minute walk along the pedestrian main drag, Via dei Calzaiuoli. Here you'll find major sights, touristy restaurants, and big crowds. My Renaissance Walk is a great introduction to this area.

Key to This Book

Sights are rated:

▲▲▲ **Don't miss**
▲▲ **Try hard to see**
▲ **Worthwhile if you can make it**
No rating **Worth knowing about**

Tourist information offices are abbreviated as **TI,** and bathrooms are **WCs.**

Like Europe, this book uses the **24-hour clock.** It's the same through 12:00 noon, then keep going: 13:00 (1:00 p.m.), 14:00 (2:00 p.m.), and so on.

For **opening times,** if a sight is listed as "May-Oct daily 9:00-16:00," it should be open from 9 a.m. until 4 p.m. from the first day of May until the last day of October (but expect exceptions).

For **updates** to this book, visit www.ricksteves.com/update. For a valuable list of reports and experiences—good and bad—from fellow travelers, check www.ricksteves.com/feedback.

North of the Duomo: Tourist activities and restaurants revolve around two main centers: the Basilica of San Lorenzo (museums and nearby markets), and the Accademia (and nearby San Marco Museum).

East of the Duomo: The landmark is the Church of Santa Croce—a major sight and a people-gathering spot. Otherwise, this is a less-touristed area, sprinkled with minor sights, and a few hotels and restaurants.

West of the Duomo: The train station (and bus station)—a 10- to 15-minute walk from the Duomo—form the western border of the historic core. The area is not so picturesque and there are few sights (besides the church of Santa Maria Novella), but it's convenient for hotels and restaurants.

South of the Arno River (Oltrarno): Less touristed and more local, it's a place of artisan workshops and car traffic. Tourists enjoy the Pitti Palace (and Boboli Gardens) and Brancacci Chapel, as well as local-filled restaurants.

Florence at a Glance

▲▲▲**Accademia** Michelangelo's *David* and powerful (unfinished) *Prisoners*. Reserve ahead or get a Firenze Card. **Hours:** Tue-Sun 8:15-18:50, closed Mon. See page 37.

▲▲▲**Duomo Museum** Underrated cathedral museum with sculptures. **Hours:** Daily 9:00-19:00. See page 89.

▲▲▲**Bargello** Underappreciated sculpture museum (Michelangelo, Donatello, Medici treasures). **Hours:** Tue-Sat 8:15-17:00, until 13:50 if there are no special exhibits; also open second and fourth Mon and first, third, and fifth Sun of each month. See page 75.

▲▲**Duomo** Gothic cathedral with colorful facade and the first dome built since ancient Roman times. **Hours:** Mon-Fri 10:00-17:00; Thu until 16:00 May and Oct, until 16:30 Nov-April; Sat 10:00-16:45, Sun 13:30-16:45. See page 110.

▲▲▲**Uffizi Gallery** Greatest collection of Italian paintings anywhere. Reserve well in advance or get a Firenze Card. **Hours:** Tue-Sun 8:15-18:35, closed Mon. See page 51.

▲▲**Museum of San Marco** Best collection anywhere of artwork by the early Renaissance master Fra Angelico. **Hours:** Tue-Fri 8:15-13:50, Sat 8:15-16:50; also open 8:15-13:50 on first, third, and fifth Mon and 8:15-16:50 on second and fourth Sun of each month. See page 116.

▲▲**Medici Chapels** Tombs of Florence's great ruling family, designed and carved by Michelangelo. **Hours:** April-Oct Tue-Sat 8:15-16:50, Nov-March 8:15-13:50; also open second and fourth Mon and first, third, and fifth Sun of each month. See page 119.

▲▲**Palazzo Vecchio** Fortified palace, once the home of the Medici family, wallpapered with history. **Hours:** Museum open April-Sept Fri-Wed 9:00-24:00, Thu 9:00-14:00; Oct-March Fri-Wed 9:00-19:00, Thu 9:00-14:00; tower keeps similar but shorter hours. See page 114.

▲▲**Galileo Science Museum** Fascinating old clocks, telescopes, maps, and Galileo's finger in a bottle. **Hours:** Wed-Mon 9:30-18:00, Tue 9:30-13:00. See page 115.

▲▲**Santa Croce Church** Precious art, tombs of famous Florentines, and Brunelleschi's Pazzi Chapel in 14th-century church. **Hours:** Mon-Sat 9:30-17:30, Sun 14:00-17:30. See page 122.

▲▲**Church of Santa Maria Novella** Thirteenth-century Dominican church with Masaccio's famous 3-D painting. **Hours:** Mon-Thu 9:00-17:30, Fri 11:00-17:30, Sat 9:00-17:00, Sun 12:00-17:00 (from 13:00 Oct-June). See page 124.

▲▲**Pitti Palace** Several museums in lavish palace plus sprawling Boboli and Bardini gardens. **Hours:** Palatine Gallery and Royal Apartments: Tue-Sun 8:15-18:50, closed Mon; Boboli and Bardini Gardens and other museums have similar (but not identical) hours. See page 127.

▲▲**Brancacci Chapel** Works of Masaccio, early Renaissance master who reinvented perspective. **Hours:** Mon and Wed-Sat 10:00-17:00, Sun 13:00-17:00, closed Tue. Reservations required, though often available on the spot. See page 131.

▲▲**San Miniato Church** Sumptuous Renaissance chapel and sacristy showing scenes of St. Benedict. **Hours:** Daily Easter-mid-Oct 8:00-20:00, off-season 8:30-13:00 & 15:30-19:00. See page 133.

▲**Climbing the Duomo's Dome** Grand view into the cathedral, close-up of dome architecture, and, after 463 steps, a glorious city vista. **Hours:** Mon-Fri 8:30-19:00, Sat 8:30-17:40, closed Sun. Reservations are required, even for Firenze Card holders. See page 111.

▲**Campanile** Bell tower with views similar to Duomo's, 50 fewer steps, and shorter lines. **Hours:** Daily 8:30-19:30. See page 20.

▲**Baptistery** Bronze doors fit to be the gates of paradise. **Hours:** Doors always viewable; interior open Mon-Sat 11:15-19:00 except first Sat of each month 8:30-14:00, Sun 8:30-14:00. See page 22.

▲**Medici-Riccardi Palace** Lorenzo the Magnificent's home, with fine art, frescoed ceilings, and Gozzoli's lovely Chapel of the Magi. **Hours:** Thu-Tue 8:30-19:00, closed Wed. See page 121.

▲**Ponte Vecchio** Famous bridge lined with gold and silver shops. **Hours:** Bridge always open (shops closed at night). See page 35.

▲**Piazzale Michelangelo** Hilltop square with stunning view of Duomo and Florence, with San Miniato Church just uphill. **Hours:** Always open. See page 133.

Casa Buonarroti Early, lesser-known works by Michelangelo. **Hours:** Wed-Mon 10:00-17:00, closed Tue. See page 123.

Daily Reminder

Sunday: The Duomo's dome, Museum of Precious Stones, and Mercato Centrale are closed.

The Baptistery's interior closes early (at 14:00).

A few sights are open only in the afternoon: Duomo (13:30-16:45), Santa Croce Church (14:00-17:30), Basilica of San Lorenzo (13:30-17:30), Brancacci Chapel (13:00-17:00), and Church of Santa Maria Novella (12:00-17:00, from 13:00 Oct-June).

The Bargello, Palazzo Davanzati, and the Medici Chapels close on the second and fourth Sundays. The Museum of San Marco is closed on the first, third, and fifth Sundays of the month.

The following sights are free and crowded on the first Sunday of the month, and reservations are not available: Uffizi, Accademia, the Pitti Palace, Bargello, Medici Chapels, and Museum of San Marco.

Monday: The biggies are closed, including the Accademia *(David)* and the Uffizi Gallery, as well as the Pitti Palace's Palatine Gallery, Royal Apartments, and Gallery of Modern Art.

The Pitti Palace, Boboli and Bardini Gardens, Argenti/Silver-works Museum, Costume Gallery, and Porcelain Museum close on the first and last Mondays. The Museum of San Marco closes on the second and fourth Mondays. The Bargello, Palazzo Davanzati, and the Medici Chapels are closed on the first, third, and fifth Mondays. San Lorenzo Market is closed Mondays in winter.

Planning Your Time

Plan your sightseeing carefully to avoid lines and work around closed days. (✪ See my sightseeing tips on page 168.) Florence is so geographically small that, even if you only had one day, you could see the biggies in a 12-hour sightseeing blitz. But let's assume you have at least three days.

Day 1: In the cool of the morning, take my Renaissance Walk. Have lunch in the old center. After lunch, art lovers will want to get a start on Florence's many sights. Choose from the Medici Chapels (Michelangelo), Santa Maria Novella, the Palazzo Vecchio, Medici-Riccardi, the Pitti Palace, Brancacci Chapel, or Santa Croce. Around 16:30 (when crowds

Target these sights on Mondays: the Duomo and its dome, Duomo Museum, Campanile, Baptistery, Medici-Riccardi Palace, Brancacci Chapel, Mercato Nuovo, Mercato Centrale, Casa Buonarroti, Galileo Science Museum, the Palazzo Vecchio, and churches (including Santa Croce and Santa Maria Novella).

Tuesday: Casa Buonarroti and the Brancacci Chapel are closed. The Galileo Science Museum closes early (13:00).

Wednesday: All sights are open, except for the Medici-Riccardi Palace and Santo Spirito Church.

Thursday: All sights are open, though the following close early: the Palazzo Vecchio (14:00) and off-season, the Duomo (16:00 May and Oct, 16:30 Nov-April).

Friday: All sights are open.

Saturday: All sights are open, but the Duomo's dome closes earlier than usual, at 17:40.

Early-Closing Warning: Some of Florence's sights close surprisingly early (by 14:00), especially off-season.

Late-Hours Relief: Many sights stay open until 18:30-19:30. The Uffizi, Accademia, the Pitti Palace, Campanile, the Palazzo Vecchio, and Duomo Museum offer regular evening hours.

die down), see the Uffizi Gallery's unforgettable paintings—reserve well in advance or get a Firenze Card. End with dinner in the old center.

Day 2: See the Accademia *(David)*—reserve in advance or get a Firenze Card. Visit the nearby Museum of San Marco (Fra Angelico). After lunch, hit the markets, shop, wander, take a bike or walking tour, or do more museum-going. Around 16:30, visit the Baptistery, climb the Campanile, and see the Duomo Museum. Then stroll to the Arno, and cross to the Oltrarno for dinner.

Day 3: Start with the Bargello (best statues), then the Galileo Science Museum. After lunch, sightsee any leftovers from the first two days. Around

16:00, take a taxi or bus to Piazzale Michelangelo for city views and the San Miniato Church. Walk back into town for dinner.

With more days, you could even fit in a day trip to Siena, Pisa, Lucca, or a Tuscan hill town.

These are busy day-plans, so be sure to schedule in slack time for picnics, laundry, people-watching, leisurely dinners, shopping, and re-charging your touristic batteries. Slow down and be open to unexpected experiences and the hospitality of the Italian people.

Trip Tips: Avoid lines by making reservations or buying a Firenze Card, and check opening hours carefully. Download my free Florence **audio tours**—covering the Renaissance Walk, the Uffizi Gallery, and the Accademia *(David)*—and take them along (✪ see page 169 for details). Do your most intense sightseeing in the morning or late afternoon to avoid heat and crowds. Stop often for gelato.

I hope you have a great trip! Traveling like a temporary local and tak-ing advantage of the information here, you'll enjoy the absolute most out of every mile, minute, and euro. I'm happy that you'll be visiting places I know and love, and meeting some of my favorite Italian people.

Happy travels! *Buon viaggio!*

Renaissance Walk

From the Duomo to the Arno River

After centuries of labor, Florence gave birth to the Renaissance. We'll start with the soaring church dome that stands as the proud symbol of the Renaissance spirit. Just opposite, you'll find the Baptistery doors that opened the Renaissance. Finally, we'll reach Florence's political center, dotted with monuments of that proud time. Great and rich as this city is, it's easily covered on foot. This walk through the top sights is less than a mile long, running from the Duomo to the Arno River.

    This walk gives an overview of the top sights in Florence—if you'd like to visit any of them in depth, ✪ see the Sights chapter for more specifics.

ORIENTATION

Getting Into Duomo Sights: You can take this walk without entering any sights, and it's free to enter the Duomo. But seeing any of the Duomo's related sights requires a €15 combo-ticket (sold at ticket office opposite Baptistery entrance; at the Campanile, Duomo crypt, and Duomo Museum; and at ticket machines in the ticket office—credit card only, requires PIN). The Duomo sights are also covered by the Firenze Card. Before entering any of the Duomo sights, you must present your Firenze Card at the ticket office opposite the Baptistery to pick up your free combo-ticket.

Duomo (Cathedral): Free, Mon-Fri 10:00-17:00; Thu until 16:00 May and Oct, until 16:30 Nov-April; Sat 10:00-16:45; Sun 13:30-16:45. A modest dress code is enforced.

Climbing the Dome: Covered by €15 combo-ticket (reserve entry time when obtaining ticket) and Firenze Card (card holders must get ticket and make reservation at ticket office opposite Baptistery); Mon-Fri 8:30-19:00, Sat 8:30-17:40, closed Sun, 463 steps.

Campanile (Giotto's Tower): Covered by €15 combo-ticket and Firenze Card, daily 8:30-19:30, last entry 40 minutes before closing, 414 steps.

Baptistery: Covered by €15 combo-ticket and Firenze Card. Interior open Mon-Sat 11:15-19:00 except first Sat of month 8:30-14:00, Sun 8:30-14:00. Entrance is at the north door (see map on page 19). Photos allowed inside. The bronze doors are on the outside, so they're always viewable and free to see.

Medici-Riccardi Palace: €7, cash only, covered by Firenze Card, Thu-Tue 8:30-19:00, closed Wed.

Orsanmichele Church: Free, daily 10:00-17:00. Upstairs museum open Mon only. The niche sculptures are always viewable from the outside.

Palazzo Vecchio: Courtyard-free; museum-€10, covered by Firenze Card; April-Sept Fri-Wed 9:00-24:00, Thu 9:00-14:00; Oct-March Fri-Wed 9:00-19:00, Thu 9:00-14:00, last entry one hour before closing.

Information: There's a TI right on Piazza del Duomo, and another one a block-and-a-half north of the Duomo at Via Cavour 1 red.

Audio Tour: You can download this chapter as a free Rick Steves audio tour (✪ see page 169).

Length of This Walk: Allow two hours for the walk, including interior visits of the Baptistery and Orsanmichele Church (but not the other sights mentioned).

With Limited Time: Skip the Medici-Riccardi Palace detour and don't go inside the Baptistery and Orsanmichele Church.

Services: Pay toilets are at the ticket office opposite the Baptistery. You can refill your water bottle at public twist-the-handle fountains at the Duomo (left side, by the dome entrance), the Palazzo Vecchio (behind the Neptune fountain), and on Ponte Vecchio.

Photography: Don't use a flash inside churches and other sights.

Eating: You'll find plenty of cafés, self-service cafeterias, bars, and gelato shops along the route. For cheap eats, try Self-Service Ristorante Leonardo or Cantinetta dei Verrazzano, a bakery/café with good *focacce* sandwiches (near the Duomo, ✪ see page 149). A fully stocked supermarket called Sapori & Dintorni is just 50 yards north of the Duomo at Borgo San Lorenzo 15 red.

Starring: Brunelleschi's dome, Ghiberti's doors, the Medici palaces, and the city of Florence—old and new.

THE WALK BEGINS

Overview

The Duomo—the cathedral with the distinctive red dome—is the center of Florence and the orientation point for this walk. If you ever get lost, home's the dome. We'll start here, see several sights in the area, and then stroll down the city's pedestrian-only main street to the Palazzo Vecchio and the Arno River. Consider prefacing this walk with a visit to the ultimate Renaissance man: Michelangelo's *David* (✪ see the Accademia Tour chapter).

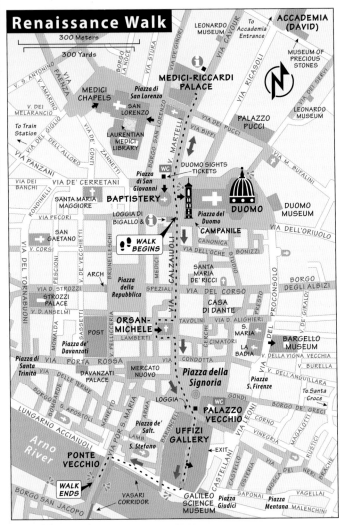

Renaissance Walk

300 Meters

300 Yards

To Train Station

LEONARDO MUSEUM

To Accademia Entrance

ACCADEMIA (DAVID)

MUSEUM OF PRECIOUS STONES

MEDICI-RICCARDI PALACE

MEDICI CHAPELS

Piazza di San Lorenzo

SAN LORENZO

LAURENTIAN MEDICI LIBRARY

LEONARDO MUSEUM

PALAZZO PUCCI

DUOMO SIGHTS TICKETS

Piazza di San Giovanni

SANTA MARIA MAGGIORE

BAPTISTERY

LOGGIA DI BIGALLO

DUOMO

DUOMO MUSEUM

Piazza del Duomo

CAMPANILE

SAN GAETANO

WALK BEGINS

CANONICA

SANTA MARIA DE' RICCI

STROZZI PALACE

ARCH

Piazza della Repubblica

VIA DEL CORSO

CASA DI DANTE

ORSAN-MICHELE

BARGELLO MUSEUM

LA BADIA

Piazza de' Davanzati

POST

DAVANZATI PALACE

MERCATO NUOVO

Piazza della Signoria

Piazza S. Firenze

To Santa Croce

Piazza di Santa Trinita

LOGGIA

PALAZZO VECCHIO

Piazza de' Salt.

S. Stefano

UFFIZI GALLERY

Arno River

PONTE VECCHIO

WALK ENDS

VASARI CORRIDOR

GALILEO SCIENCE MUSEUM

Piazza Giudici

Piazza Mentana

> *Stand in front of the Duomo as you get your historical bearings.*

The Florentine Renaissance (1400-1550)

In the 13th and 14th centuries, Florence was a powerful center of banking, trading, and textile manufacturing. The resulting wealth fertilized the cultural soil. Then came the Black Death in 1348. Nearly half the population died, but the infrastructure remained strong, and the city rebuilt better than ever. Led by Florence's chief family—the art-crazy Medici—and propelled by the naturally aggressive and creative spirit of the Florentines, it's no wonder that the long-awaited Renaissance finally took root here.

The Renaissance—the "rebirth" of Greek and Roman culture that swept across Europe—started around 1400 and lasted about 150 years. In politics, the Renaissance meant democracy; in science, a renewed interest in exploring nature. The general mood was optimistic and "humanistic," with a confidence in the power of the individual.

In medieval times, poverty and ignorance had made life "nasty, brutish, and short" (for lack of a better cliché). The church was the people's opiate, and their lives were only a preparation for a happier time in heaven after leaving this miserable vale of tears.

Medieval art was the church's servant. The noblest art form was architecture—churches themselves—and other arts were considered most worthwhile if they embellished the house of God. Painting and sculpture were narrative and symbolic, designed to tell Bible stories to the devout and illiterate masses.

As prosperity rose in Florence, so did people's confidence in life and themselves. Middle-class craftsmen, merchants, and bankers felt they could control their own destinies, rather than be at the whim of nature. They found much in common with the ancient Greeks and Romans, who valued logic and reason above superstition and blind faith.

Renaissance art was a return to the realism and balance of Greek and Roman sculpture and architecture. Domes and round arches replaced Gothic spires and pointed arches. In painting and sculpture, Renaissance artists strove for realism. Merging art and science, they used mathematics, the laws of perspective, and direct observation of nature to paint the world, 3-D on a flat surface.

This was not an anti-Christian movement, though it was a logical and scientific age. Artists saw themselves as an extension of God's creative powers. The church even supported the Renaissance and commissioned many of its greatest works—for instance, Raphael frescoed images of Plato and Aristotle on the walls of the Vatican. But for the first time in Europe since Roman times, there were rich laymen who wanted art simply for art's sake.

After 1,000 years of waiting, the smoldering fires of Europe's classical heritage burst into flames right here in Florence.

▶ *The dome of the Duomo is best viewed just to the right of the facade, from the corner of the pedestrian-only street.*

The Duomo—Florence's Cathedral

The dome of Florence's cathedral—visible from all over the city—inspired Florentines to do great things. (Most recently, it inspired the city to make the area around the cathedral delightfully traffic-free.) The big church itself (called the Duomo) is Gothic, built in the Middle Ages by architects who left it unfinished.

Think of the confidence of the age: The Duomo was built with a big hole in its roof, just waiting for a grand dome to cover it. They could envision it—but the technology needed to create such a dome had yet to be invented. *No problema.* The Florentines knew that someone would soon be able to handle the challenge. In the 1400s, the architect Filippo Brunelleschi was called on to finish the job. Brunelleschi capped the church Roman-style—with a tall, self-supporting dome as grand as the ancient Pantheon's (which he had studied).

He used a dome within a dome. First, he built the grand white skeletal ribs, which you can see, then filled them in with interlocking bricks in a herringbone pattern. The dome grew upward like an igloo, supporting itself as it proceeded from the base. When the ribs reached the top, Brunelleschi

Brunelleschi's dome atop the medieval Duomo

The Duomo facade—glorious or gaudy?

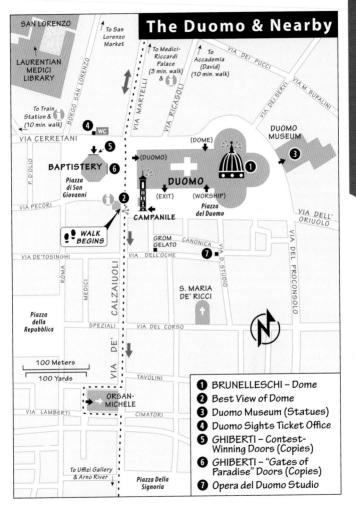

The Duomo & Nearby

SAN LORENZO

LAURENTIAN MEDICI LIBRARY

To San Lorenzo Market

To Medici-Riccardi Palace (3 min. walk) &

To Accademia (David) (10 min. walk)

VIA DEI PUCCI

VIA M. BUFALINI

VIA DEL SERVI

BORGO SAN LORENZO

VIA MARTELLI

VIA RICASOLI

To Train Station & (10 min. walk)

VIA CERRETANI

❹ WC

P. D'OLIO

❺

BAPTISTERY ❻

Piazza di San Giovanni

VIA PECORI

❷

(DUOMO)

(DOME)

✚ DUOMO

DUOMO MUSEUM

❸

❶

(EXIT)

(WORSHIP)

CAMPANILE

Piazza del Duomo

VIA DELL' ORIUOLO

WALK BEGINS

GROM GELATO

CANONICA

VIA DELL'OCHE

❼ ▪

VIA DE'TOSINGHI

ROMA

MEDICI

CALZAIUOLI

VIA D. STUDIO

VIA DEL PROCONSOLO

Piazza della Repubblica

SPEZIALI

VIA DEL CORSO

S. MARIA DE' RICCI ✝

N

100 Meters

100 Yards

TAVOLINI

VIA DE'

ORSAN-MICHELE

VIA LAMBERTI

CIMATORI

To Uffizi Gallery & Arno River

Piazza Della Signoria

❶ BRUNELLESCHI – Dome
❷ Best View of Dome
❸ Duomo Museum (Statues)
❹ Duomo Sights Ticket Office
❺ GHIBERTI – Contest-Winning Doors (Copies)
❻ GHIBERTI – "Gates of Paradise" Doors (Copies)
❼ Opera del Duomo Studio

arched them in and fixed them in place with the cupola at the top. His dome, built in only 14 years, was the largest since Rome's Pantheon.

Brunelleschi's dome was the wonder of the age, the model for many domes to follow, from St. Peter's to the US Capitol. People gave it the ultimate compliment, saying, "Not even the ancients could have done it." Michelangelo, setting out to construct the dome of St. Peter's, drew inspiration from the dome of Florence. He said, "I'll make its sister...bigger, but not more beautiful."

The church's facade looks old, but is actually Neo-Gothic—only from 1870. The facade was rushed to completion (about 600 years after the building began) to celebrate Italian unity, here in the city that for a few years served as the young country's capital. Its "retro" look captures the feel of the original medieval facade, with green, white, and pink marble sheets that cover the brick construction; Gothic (pointed) arches; and three horizontal stories decorated with mosaics and statues. Still, the facade is generally ridiculed. (While one of this book's authors thinks it's the most beautiful church facade this side of heaven, the other one naively agrees with those who call it "the cathedral in pajamas.")

The cavernous interior feels bare after being cleaned out during the Neoclassical age and by the terrible flood of 1966. It's free to go inside but not worth a long wait; lines generally disappear late in the day. For a brief tour of the interior, ✪ see page 110. To climb the dome, enter from outside the church on the north side (✪ see page 111).

Campanile (Giotto's Tower)

The bell tower (to the right of the cathedral's front) offers an easier, less crowded, and faster climb than the Duomo's dome, though the unobstructed views from the Duomo are better. Giotto, like any good Renaissance genius (even though he was pre-Renaissance), wore several artistic hats. He's considered the father of modern painting, as well as being the architect of this 270-foot-tall bell tower for the Duomo, built two centuries before the age of Michelangelo. In his day, Giotto was called the ugliest man to ever walk the streets of Florence, but he designed what many call the most beautiful bell tower in all of Europe.

The bell tower served as a sculpture gallery for Renaissance artists—notice Donatello's four prophets on the side that faces the piazza (west). These are copies—the originals are at the wonderful Duomo Museum, just behind the church. If you visit the Duomo Museum, you'll see Donatello's

Spanning the centuries: 11th-century Baptistery, 14th-century church and tower, 15th-century dome, 19th-century facade

Habakkuk and *Jeremiah* and the hexagonal panels that ring the Campanile. You'll also get a close-up look at Brunelleschi's wooden model of his dome, Ghiberti's doors (described next), and a late *Pietà* by Michelangelo. A couple of blocks south of the Duomo, at the Opera del Duomo Studio, workers sculpt and restore statues for the cathedral (Via dello Studio 23a—see location on map on page 19; you can peek in through the doorway).

▶ *The Baptistery is the small octagonal building in front of the church. If you decide to go inside, you can get a ticket at the office across the piazza (Firenze Card holders need to get a ticket at the ticket office). If you just want to look at the exterior doors, there's no charge, of course.*

Baptistery and Ghiberti's Bronze Doors

Florence's Baptistery is dear to the soul of the city. In medieval and Renaissance times, the locals—eager to link themselves to the classical past—believed (wrongly) that this was a Roman building. It is, however, Florence's oldest building—a thousand years old. And for a thousand years, most of the city's festivals and parades have either started or ended here.

North Doors: The Baptistery's bronze doors bring us out of the Middle Ages and into the Renaissance. Some say the Renaissance began precisely in the year 1401, when Florence staged a competition to find the best artist to create the Baptistery's north entrance, where tourists go in. (These are copies; the originals are in the Duomo Museum.) Florence had strong civic spirit, with different guilds (powerful trade associations) and merchant groups embellishing their city with superb art. All the greats entered the contest, but 25-year-old Lorenzo Ghiberti won easily, beating out heavyweights such as Brunelleschi (who, after losing the Baptistery gig,

Baptistery doors—the "Gates of Paradise"

Jacob and Esau—receding arches create 3-D

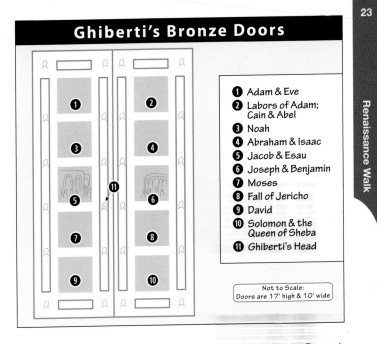

Ghiberti's Bronze Doors

1. Adam & Eve
2. Labors of Adam; Cain & Abel
3. Noah
4. Abraham & Isaac
5. Jacob & Esau
6. Joseph & Benjamin
7. Moses
8. Fall of Jericho
9. David
10. Solomon & the Queen of Sheba
11. Ghiberti's Head

Not to Scale:
Doors are 17' high & 10' wide

was free to go to Rome, study the Pantheon, and later design the Duomo's dome). The original entries of Brunelleschi and Ghiberti are in the Bargello, where you can judge them for yourself (✪ see page 85).

Later, in 1425, Ghiberti was given another commission, for the **east doors** (facing the church). This time there was literally no contest. The bronze panels of these doors added a whole new dimension to art—depth. Michelangelo said these doors were fit to be the "Gates of Paradise." (These panels are copies; the originals are in the nearby Duomo Museum. For more detailed descriptions of the panels, ✪ see page 93.) Here we see how the Renaissance masters merged art and science. Realism was in, and Renaissance artists used math, illusion, and dissection to create it.

Find the Jacob and Esau panel (just above eye level on the left). The receding arches, floor tiles, and banisters create a background for a realistic scene. The figures in the foreground stand and move like real people,

Baptistery interior's *Last Judgment* mosaic: Christ gives the ultimate thumbs-up and thumbs-down

telling the Bible story with human details. Amazingly, this spacious, 3-D scene is made from bronze only a few inches deep.

Ghiberti spent 27 years (1425-1452) working on these panels. That's him in the center of the door frame, atop the second row of panels—the head on the left with the shiny male-pattern baldness.

Inside the Baptistery: The interior features a fine example of pre-Renaissance mosaic art (1200s-1300s) in the Byzantine style. Workers from St. Mark's in Venice came here to make the remarkable ceiling mosaics (of Venetian glass) in the late 1200s.

The Last Judgment on the ceiling gives us a glimpse of the medieval worldview. Life was a preparation for the afterlife, when you would be judged and saved, or damned, with no in-between. Christ, peaceful and reassuring, would bless those at his right hand with heaven (thumbs up) and send those on his left to hell (the ultimate thumbs-down), to be tortured by demons and gnashed between the teeth of monsters. This hellish scene looks like something right out of the *Inferno* by Dante, who was dipped into the baptismal waters right here.

The rest of the ceiling mosaics tell the history of the world, from Adam and Eve (over the north/entrance doors, top row) to Noah and the Flood (over south doors, top row), to the life of Christ (second row) to the life, ministry, and eventual beheading of John the Baptist (bottom row, all around), all bathed in the golden glow of pre-Renaissance heaven.

▶ *Before we head south to the river, gaze a block north up Via de' Martelli (which becomes Via Cavour—the street that goes straight up between the Duomo and Baptistery). At the intersection with Via dei Pucci is the imposing, brown stone...*

Medici-Riccardi Palace

This was the home of the Medici, the rich banking family who ruled Renaissance Florence. Studying this grand Florentine palace, you'll notice fortified lower walls and elegance limited to the fancy upper stories. The Medici may have been the local Rockefellers, but having self-made wealth rather than actual noble blood, they were always a bit defensive. The Greek motifs along the eaves highlight the palace's Renaissance roots. Back then, rather than having parking spots, grand buildings came with iron rings to which you'd tether your horse.

If you visit the palace, you can either view the courtyard for free (through the iron gate) or pay admission to go inside for a quintessential Florentine palazzo with the sumptuously painted Chapel of the Magi.

⊗ See the Medici-Riccardi Palace listing on page 121.

▶ *Though we won't visit them on this walk, one block west of here are the Basilica of San Lorenzo (⊗ page 118) and Medici Chapels (⊗ page 119); nearby, surrounding Mercato Centrale, are the leather-and-knickknack stalls of San Lorenzo Market. For now, return to the Duomo and continue south, entering the pedestrian-only street that runs from here toward the Arno River.*

Via de' Calzaiuoli

The pedestrian-only Via de' Calzaiuoli (kahlts-ay-WOH-lee) is lined with shops that cater to the mobs of tourists. This street has always been the main axis of the city, and was part of the ancient Roman grid plan that became Florence. In medieval times, this street connected the religious center (where we are now) with the political center (where we're heading), a five-minute walk away. In recent years, this historic core has been transformed from noisy traffic jams to a pleasant place to stroll, people-watch, window-shop, lick the drips on your gelato cone, and wonder why American cities can't become more pedestrian-friendly.

And speaking of gelato...**Grom,** which keeps its *gelati* in covered metal bins, the old-fashioned way, is just a half-block detour away (take your first left, to Via delle Oche 24 red). Or you could drop by any of the several nearby gelato shops. *Perché no?* (Why not?)

Continue down Via de' Calzaiuoli. Two blocks down from the Baptistery, look right on Via degli Speziali to see a triumphal arch that marks **Piazza della Repubblica.** The arch celebrates the unification of Italy in 1870 and stands as a reminder that, in ancient Roman times, this piazza was the city center. For more on this square, ✪ see page 113.

▶ *A block farther, at the intersection with Via Orsanmichele, is the...*

Orsanmichele Church—Florence's Medieval Roots

The Orsanmichele Church provides an interesting look at Florentine values. It's a combo church/granary. Originally, this was an open loggia (covered porch) with a huge grain warehouse upstairs. The arches of the loggia were artfully filled in (14th century), and the building gained a new purpose—as a church. This was prime real estate on what had become the main drag between the cathedral and palace.

The 14 niches in the walls feature remarkable-in-their-day statues, paid by the city's rising middle class of merchants and their 21 guilds. Florence in 1400 was a republic, a government working for the interests not of a king, but of these guilds (much as modern America is controlled by and caters to corporate interests). The guilds commissioned statues as PR gestures, hiring the finest artists of the generation. As the statues were done over several decades, they function as a textbook of the evolution of Florentine art.

Orsanmichele—staid late-medieval saints

Donatello's bold, Renaissance *St. George*

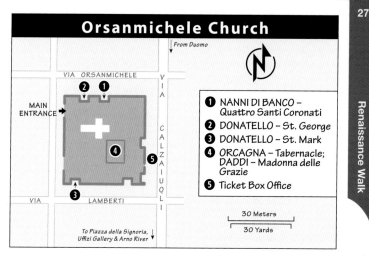

Orsanmichele Church

From Duomo

VIA ORSANMICHELE

2 1

MAIN ENTRANCE →

VIA CALZAIUQLI

4

5

VIA LAMBERTI

3

To Piazza della Signoria,
Uffizi Gallery & Arno River

1 NANNI DI BANCO – Quattro Santi Coronati
2 DONATELLO – St. George
3 DONATELLO – St. Mark
4 ORCAGNA – Tabernacle; DADDI – Madonna delle Grazie
5 Ticket Box Office

30 Meters

30 Yards

Orsanmichele Exterior

In earlier Gothic times, statues were set deep into church niches, simply embellishing the house of God. Here at the Orsanmichele Church, we see statues—as restless as man on the verge of the Renaissance—stepping out from the protection of the Church.

▶ *Head up Via Orsanmichele and circle the church exterior counterclock-wise to enjoy the statues. While these are all copies, you can see the originals in the museum on the church's top floor and the most famous of the statues (St. George) in the Bargello. In the third niche is...*

Nanni di Banco's *Quattro Santi Coronati* (c. 1415-1417)

These four early Christians were sculptors martyred by the Roman em-peror Diocletian because they refused to sculpt pagan gods. They seem to be contemplating the consequences of the fatal decision they're about to make. Beneath some of the niches, you'll find the symbol of the guilds that paid for the art. Art historians differ here. Some think the work was com-missioned by the carpenters' and masons' guild. Others contend it was by the guys who did discount circumcisions.

▶ *While Banco's saints are deep in the church's niche, the next statue feels ready to step out. Just to the right is...*

Donatello's *St. George* (c. 1417)

George is alert, perched on the edge of his niche, scanning the horizon for dragons and announcing the new age with its new outlook. His knitted brow shows there's a drama unfolding. Sure, he's anxious, but he's also self-assured. Comparing this Renaissance-style *St. George* to *Quattro Santi Coronati,* you can psychoanalyze the heady changes under way. This is humanism.

This *St. George* is a copy of the original (located in the Bargello, and described in the Bargello Tour chapter).

The small carving below the statue reminds viewers that this statue was brought to you by the sword and armor makers' guild. Art historians consider Donatello's delightful little S-shaped figure on the right a breakthrough in realism.

▶ *Continue counterclockwise around the church (bypassing the entrance for now), all the way to the opposite side.*

Donatello's *St. Mark* (1411-1413)

The evangelist cradles his gospel in his strong, veined hand and gazes out, resting his weight on the right leg while bending the left. Though subtle, St. Mark's *contrapposto* pose (weight on one foot) was the first seen since antiquity. Commissioned by the linen-sellers' guild, the statue has elaborately detailed robes that drape around the natural contours of his weighty body. When the guild first saw the statue, they thought the oversized head and torso made it top-heavy. Only after it was lifted into its raised niche did Donatello's cleverly designed proportions look right—and the guild accepted it. Eighty years after young Donatello carved this statue, a teenage Michelangelo Buonarroti stood here and marveled at it.

▶ *Backtrack to the entrance and go inside.*

Orsanmichele Interior

Step into Florence, circa 1350. The church does not have a typical nave because it was adapted from a granary. Look for the pillars (on the left) with rectangular holes in them about three feet off the ground. These were once used as chutes for delivering grain from the storage rooms upstairs. Look up to see the rings hanging from the ceiling, likely used to make pulleys for lifting grain, and the iron bars spanning the vaults for support.

The fine **tabernacle** is by Andrea Orcagna. Notice how it was designed exactly for this space: Like the biggest Christmas tree possible, it's

Donatello's *St. Mark* on Orsanmichele

Gothic tabernacle inside Orsanmichele

capped by an angel whose head touches the ceiling. Take in the Gothic tabernacle's medieval elegance. What it lacks in depth and realism it makes up for in color, with an intricate assemblage of marble, glass, gold, and expensive lapis lazuli. Florence had just survived the terrible bubonic plague of 1348, which killed half the population. The elaborate tabernacle was built to display Bernardo Daddi's *Madonna delle Grazie,* which received plague survivors' grateful prayers of thanks—*grazie.* While it's great to see art in museums, it's even better to enjoy it in its original setting—"in situ"—where the artist intended it to be seen. When you view similar altarpieces out of context in the Uffizi, think back to the candlelit medieval atmosphere that surrounds this altarpiece.

Upstairs is a free museum (open only Mon 10:00-17:00) displaying most of the originals of the statues you just saw outside. They represent virtually every big name in pre-Michelangelo Florentine sculpture: Donatello, Ghiberti, Brunelleschi, Giambologna, and more.

The church hosts atmospheric evening concerts; same-day tickets are sold on the day of the concert from the door facing Via de' Calzaiuoli (see Orsanmichele Church map). You can also book tickets here for the Uffizi and Accademia.

▶ *The Bargello, with Florence's best collection of sculpture, is a few blocks east, down Via dei Tavolini. (✪ See the Bargello Tour chapter.) But let's continue down the mall 50 more yards, to the huge and historic square called...*

Piazza della Signoria

What a view! The main civic center of Florence, Piazza della Signoria is dominated by the Palazzo Vecchio, the Uffizi Gallery, and the marble greatness of old Florence littering its cobbles. Piazza della Signoria still vibrates with the echoes of Florence's past—executions, riots, and great celebrations. There's even Roman history: Look for the **chart** showing the ancient city (on a waist-high, freestanding display to your right as you enter the square). Today, it's a tourist's world, with pigeons, selfie sticks, horse buggies, and tired hubbies. If it would make your tired hubby or weary wife

Palazzo Vecchio—Florence's Town Hall, cradle of early democracy, and home of Cosimo Medici

Palazzo Vecchio & Nearby

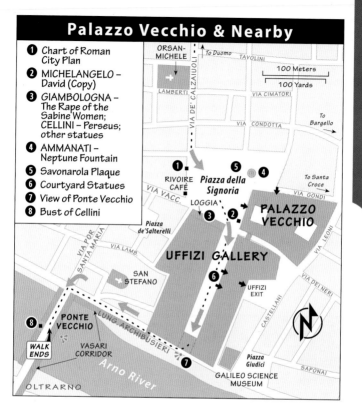

1 Chart of Roman City Plan

2 MICHELANGELO – David (Copy)

3 GIAMBOLOGNA – The Rape of the Sabine Women; CELLINI – Perseus; other statues

4 AMMANATI – Neptune Fountain

5 Savonarola Plaque

6 Courtyard Statues

7 View of Ponte Vecchio

8 Bust of Cellini

come to life, stop in at the expensive **Rivoire** café to enjoy its fine desserts, pudding-thick hot chocolate, and the best view seats in town.

Before you towers the Palazzo Vecchio, the palatial Town Hall of the Medici—a fortress designed to contain riches and survive the many riots that went with local politics. The windows are just beyond the reach of angry stones, and the tower was a handy lookout post. Justice was doled out sternly on this square. Until 1873, Michelangelo's **David** stood where you see the replica today. The original was damaged in a 1527 riot (when a bench thrown from a palace window knocked its left arm off), but remained here for several centuries, vulnerable to erosion and pollution until it was moved indoors for its own protection.

Step past the fake *David* through the front door into the Palazzo Vecchio's courtyard (free). This palace was Florence's symbol of civic power. You're surrounded by art for art's sake—a cherub frivolously marks the courtyard's center, and ornate stuccoes and frescoes decorate the walls and columns. Such luxury represented a big change 500 years ago. For more on this palace, ✪ see page 114.

▶ *Back outside, check out the statue-filled...*

Loggia dei Lanzi (a.k.a. Loggia della Signoria)

The loggia, once a forum for public debate, was perfect for a city that prided itself on its democratic traditions. But later, when the Medici figured that good art was more desirable than free speech, it was turned into an outdoor sculpture gallery. Notice the squirming Florentine themes—conquest, domination, rape, and decapitation. The statues lining the back are Roman originals brought back to Florence by a Medici when his villa in Rome was sold. Two statues in the front deserve a closer look.

The Rape of the Sabine Women, with its pulse-quickening rhythm of muscles, is from the restless Mannerist period, which followed the stately and confident Renaissance (c. 1583). The sculptor, Giambologna,

The Rape of the Sabine Women, in the Loggia   *Perseus* recalls the classical world.

proved his mastery of the medium by sculpting three entangled bodies from one piece of marble. The composition is best viewed from below and in front. The relief panel below shows a wider view of the terrible scene. Note what looks like an IV tube on the arm of the horrified husband. It's an electrified wire that effectively keeps the pigeons away. (In the Accademia, you can see the original plaster model of this statue that was used to guide Giambologna's workers in helping him create it.)

Benvenuto Cellini's **Perseus** (1545-1553), the loggia's most note-worthy piece, shows the Greek hero who decapitated the snake-headed Medusa. They say Medusa was so ugly she turned humans who looked at her to stone—though one of this book's authors thinks she's kinda cute.

▶ *Cross the square to the big fountain of* Neptune *by Bartolomeo Ammanati that Florentines (including Michelangelo) consider a huge waste of marble—though one of this book's authors...*

The guy on the horse, to the left, is Cosimo I, one of the post-Renaissance Medici. Find the round bronze plaque on the ground 10 steps in front of the fountain.

Savonarola Plaque

The Medici family was briefly thrown from power by an austere monk named Savonarola, who made Florence a constitutional republic. He organized huge rallies lit by roaring bonfires here on the square where he preached. While children sang hymns, the devout brought their rich "vanities" (such as paintings, musical instruments, and playing cards) and threw them into the flames.

But not everyone wanted a return to the medieval past. Encouraged by the pope, the Florentines fought back and arrested Savonarola. For two days, they tortured him, trying unsuccessfully to persuade him to see their side of things. Finally, on the very spot where Savonarola's followers had built bonfires of vanities, the monk was burned. The bronze plaque, engraved in Italian *("Qui dove...")*, reads, "Here, Girolamo Savonarola and his Dominican brothers were hanged and burned" in the year "MCCCCXCVIII" (1498). Soon after, the Medici returned to power, ending Savonarola's theocracy. The Renaissance picked up where it left off.

▶ *Stay cool, we have 200 yards to go. Follow the gaze of the fake* David *into the courtyard of the two-tone horseshoe-shaped building.*

Uffizi Courtyard—The Renaissance Hall of Fame

The top floor of this building, known as the *uffizi* (offices) during Medici days, is filled with the greatest collection of Florentine painting anywhere. It's one of Europe's top four or five art galleries (✪ see the Uffizi Gallery Tour chapter).

The Uffizi courtyard, filled with merchants and hustling young artists, is watched over by 19th-century statues of the great figures of the Renaissance. Tourists zero in on the visual accomplishments of the era, but let's pay tribute to the many other accomplishments of the Renaissance as well, as we wander through Florence's Hall of Fame.

▶ *Stroll down the left side of the courtyard from the Palazzo Vecchio to the river, noticing the following greats.*

Lorenzo the Magnificent, the Medici ruler, was a great art patron and cunning power broker. Excelling in everything except modesty, he set the tone for the Renaissance. His statue is tucked under the arcade, by an Uffizi doorway.

Giotto, holding the plan to the city's bell tower—named for him— was the great pre-Renaissance artist whose paintings foretold the future of Italian art.

Donatello, the sculptor who served as a role model for Michelangelo, holds a hammer and chisel.

Alberti wrote a famous book, *On Painting,* which taught early Renaissance artists the mathematics of perspective.

Lorenzo the Magnificent outside the Uffizi

Machiavelli—the ends justify the means

Leonardo da Vinci was a scientist, sculptor, musician, engineer... and not a bad painter either. This well-roundedness marked the epitome of a Renaissance genius.

Michelangelo ponders the universe and/or stifles a belch.

Dante, with the laurel-leaf crown and lyre of a poet, says, "I am the father of the Italian language." He was the first Italian to write a popular work *(The Divine Comedy)* in non-Latin, using the Florentine dialect, which soon became "Italian" throughout the country.

The poet **Petrarch** wears laurel leaves from Greece, a robe from Rome, and a belt from Walmart.

Boccaccio wrote *The Decameron,* stories told to pass the time during the 1348 Black Death. He helped popularize literature in the people's language rather than Latin.

Machiavelli looks like he's deviously hatching a plot—his book *The Prince* taught that the end justifies the means, paving the way for the slick-and-cunning "Machiavellian" politics of today.

Vespucci (in the corner) was an explorer who gave his first name, Amerigo, to a fledgling New World.

Galileo (in the other corner) holds the humble telescope he used to spot the moons of Jupiter.

▶ *Pause at the Arno River, overlooking...*

Ponte Vecchio

Before you is Ponte Vecchio (Old Bridge). A bridge has spanned this narrowest part of the Arno since Roman times. While Rome "fell," Florence really didn't, remaining a bustling trade center along the river. To get into the exclusive little park below (on the north bank), you'll need to join the Florence rowing club.

▶ *Finish your walk by hiking to the center of the bridge.*

A fine **bust** of the great goldsmith Cellini graces the central point of the bridge. This statue is a reminder that, in the 1500s, the Medici booted out the bridge's butchers and tanners and installed the gold- and silversmiths who still tempt visitors to this day. This is a very romantic spot late at night (when lovers gather, and a top-notch street musician performs).

Look up to notice the Vasari Corridor, the protected and elevated passageway that led the Medici from the Palazzo Vecchio through the Uffizi, across Ponte Vecchio, and up to the immense Pitti Palace, four blocks

Spanning the Arno since 1345, Ponte Vecchio is barnacled with merchants' shops.

beyond the bridge. During World War II, the Nazi occupiers were ordered to blow up Ponte Vecchio. An art-loving German consul intervened and saved the bridge. The buildings at either end were destroyed, leaving the bridge impassable but intact.

▶ *From the Duomo to the Arno, we've taken in sights from Florence's medieval roots and Renaissance greats. And we saw how that sophistication has continued in the stylish Florence of today. Now that you've had a full meal of high culture, finish it off with a dessert of the world's finest gelato. Enjoy.*

Accademia Tour: Michelangelo's *David*

Galleria dell'Accademia

One of Europe's great thrills is actually seeing Michelangelo's *David* in the flesh. Seventeen feet high, gleaming white, and exalted by a halo-like dome over his head, *David* rarely disappoints, even for those with high expectations. And the Accademia doesn't stop there. With a handful of other Michelangelo statues, some fine Renaissance paintings, a Giambologna masterpiece, and even a musical instruments collection, it makes for an uplifting visit that isn't overwhelming. *David,* a must-see on any visit to Florence, is always jammed with visitors. Plan carefully to minimize your time in line.

ORIENTATION

Cost: €12.50 (or €8 if there's no special exhibit), additional €4 fee for recommended reservation, free and crowded on the first Sun of the month, covered by Firenze Card.

Hours: Tue-Sun 8:15-18:50, closed Mon.

Avoiding Lines: In peak season (April-Oct), it's smart to buy a Firenze Card or reserve at least several days ahead (✪ see page 169 for info on both options). Those with reservations or the Firenze Card line up at the entrance labeled *Reserved*. (Note that the *Reserved* entrance is split into two queues—groups and individuals.) If you show up without a reservation or Firenze Card, and there's a long line, the My Accademia Libreria reservation office (across the street from the exit) might have same-day reservations available (€4 fee). On off-season weekdays (Nov-March) before 8:30 or after 16:00, you can sometimes get in with no reservation and no lines. The museum is most crowded on Sun, Tue, and from 11:00 to 13:00.

Getting There: It's at Via Ricasoli 60, a 10-minute walk northeast of the Duomo.

Information: Reservation tel. 055-294-883, www.polomuseale.firenze.it.

Tour: A €6 audioguide (€10/2 people) is available in the ticket lobby.
✪ Download my free Accademia **audio tour.**

Length of This Tour: *David* and the *Prisoners* can be seen in 30 minutes. Allow another 30 minutes to explore the rest.

Baggage Check: The museum has no bag-check service. Large backpacks are not allowed.

Services: The WCs are downstairs near the entrance/exit. There's a small book/gift shop just inside the entrance and a larger one near the exit.

Photography: No flash photography.

Cuisine Art: Gelateria Carabè, popular for its sumptuous *granite* (fresh-fruit Italian ices) is a block toward the Duomo, at Via Ricasoli 60 red. Picnickers can stock up at Il Centro Supermercati/sandwich bar, a half-block north at Via Ricasoli 109. La Mescita Fiaschetteria serves inexpensive pasta and sandwiches, around the Accademia's south corner at Via degli Alfani 70 red.

Starring: Michelangelo's *David* and *Prisoners*.

Accademia Overview

Not to Scale

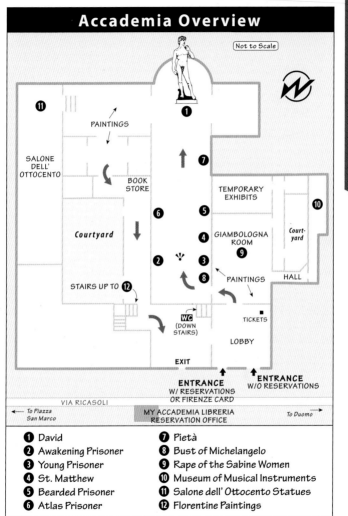

PAINTINGS

11

SALONE
DELL'
OTTOCENTO

BOOK
STORE

Courtyard

1 David

7 Pietà

STAIRS UP TO **12**

TEMPORARY
EXHIBITS

10

Court-
yard

6 **5**

4 GIAMBOLOGNA
ROOM
9

2 **3**

8

PAINTINGS

HALL

WC
(DOWN
STAIRS)

TICKETS

LOBBY

EXIT

ENTRANCE
W/ RESERVATIONS
OR FIRENZE CARD

ENTRANCE
W/O RESERVATIONS

VIA RICASOLI

← To Piazza
San Marco

MY ACCADEMIA LIBRERIA
RESERVATION OFFICE

To Duomo →

1 David	**7** Pietà
2 Awakening Prisoner	**8** Bust of Michelangelo
3 Young Prisoner	**9** Rape of the Sabine Women
4 St. Matthew	**10** Museum of Musical Instruments
5 Bearded Prisoner	**11** Salone dell' Ottocento Statues
6 Atlas Prisoner	**12** Florentine Paintings

THE TOUR BEGINS

▶ *From the entrance lobby, show your ticket, turn left, and look right down the long hall with* David *at the far end, under a halo-like dome. Yes, you're really here. With* David *presiding at the "altar," the* Prisoners *lining the "nave," and hordes of "pilgrims" crowding in to look, you've arrived at Florence's "cathedral of humanism."*

Start with the ultimate...

David (1501-1504)

When you look into the eyes of Michelangelo's *David,* you're looking into the eyes of Renaissance Man. This 17-foot-tall symbol of divine victory over evil represents a new century and a whole new Renaissance outlook. This is the age of Columbus and classicism, Galileo and Gutenberg, Luther and Leonardo—of Florence and the Renaissance.

In 1501, Michelangelo Buonarroti, a 26-year-old Florentine, was commissioned to carve a large-scale work for the Duomo. He was given a block of marble that other sculptors had rejected as too tall, shallow, and flawed to be of any value. But Michelangelo picked up his hammer and chisel, knocked a knot off what became *David*'s heart, and started to work.

The figure comes from a Bible story. The Israelites, God's chosen people, are surrounded by barbarian warriors led by a brutish giant named Goliath. The giant challenges the Israelites to send out someone to fight him. Everyone is afraid except for one young shepherd boy—David. Armed only with a sling, which he's thrown over his shoulder, David gathers five smooth stones from the stream and faces Goliath.

The statue captures David as he's sizing up his enemy. He stands relaxed but alert, leaning on one leg in a classical pose known as *contrapposto*. In his powerful right hand, he fondles the handle of the sling, ready to fling a stone at the giant. His gaze is steady—searching with intense concentration, but also with extreme confidence. Michelangelo has caught the precise moment when David is saying to himself, "I can take this guy."

Note that while the label on *David* indicates that he's already slain the giant, the current director of the Accademia believes, as I do, that Michelangelo has portrayed David facing the giant. Unlike most depictions of David after the kill, this sculpture does not show the giant's severed head. There's also a question of exactly how David's sling would work.

17-foot-tall, 12,000-pound symbol of Renaissance optimism, balanced atop a fragile right ankle

David, David, David, and *David*

Several Italian masters produced iconic sculptures of David—all of them different. Compare and contrast the artists' styles. How many ways can you slay a giant?

Donatello's *David* (1430, Bargello, Florence)
Donatello's *David* is young and graceful, casually gloating over the head of Goliath, almost Gothic in its elegance and smooth lines. While he has a similar weight-on-one-leg *(contrapposto)* stance as Michelangelo's later version, Donatello's *David* seems feminine rather than masculine. (For further description, ✪ see page 82 of the Bargello Tour chapter.)

Andrea del Verrocchio's *David* (c. 1470, Bargello, Florence)
Wearing a military skirt and armed with a small sword, Verrocchio's *David* is just a boy. The statue is only four feet tall—dwarfed by Michelangelo's monumental version. (For more, ✪ see page 81 of the Bargello Tour chapter.)

Michelangelo's *David* (1501-1504, Accademia, Florence)
Michelangelo's *David* is pure Renaissance: massive, heroic in size, and superhuman in strength and power. The tensed right hand, which grips a stone in readiness to

hurl at Goliath, is more powerful than any human hand. It's symbolic of divine strength. A model of perfection, Michelangelo's *David* is far larger and grander than we mere mortals. We know he'll win. Renaissance Man has arrived.

Gian Lorenzo Bernini's *David* (1623, Borghese Museum, Rome)
Flash forward more than a century. In this self-portrait, 25-year-old

Bernini is ready to take on the world, slay the pretty-boy Davids of the Renaissance, and invent Baroque. Unlike Michelangelo's rational, cool, restrained *David*, Bernini's is a doer: passionate, engaged, dramatic. While Renaissance *David* is simple and unadorned—carrying only a sling—Baroque Dave is "cluttered" with a braided sling, a hairy pouch, flowing cloth, and discarded armor. Bernini's *David*, with his tousled hair and set mouth, is one of us; the contest is less certain than with the other three *David*s.

To sum up: Donatello's *David* represents the first inkling of the Renaissance; Verrocchio's is early Renaissance in miniature; Michelangelo's is textbook Renaissance; and Bernini's is the epitome of Baroque.

Is he holding the stone in his right or left hand? Does the right hand hold the sling's pouch or the retention handle of a sling? Scholars debate Sling Theory endlessly.

David is a symbol of Renaissance optimism. He's no brute. He's a civilized, thinking individual who can grapple with and overcome problems. He needs no armor, only his God-given body and wits. Look at his right hand, with the raised veins and strong, relaxed fingers—many complained that it was too big and overdeveloped. But this is the hand of a man with the strength of God. No mere boy could slay the giant. But David, powered by God, could...and did.

Originally, the statue was commissioned to stand along the southern roofline of the Duomo. But during the three years it took to sculpt, they decided instead to place it guarding the entrance of Town Hall—the Palazzo Vecchio. (If the relationship between *David*'s head and body seems a bit out of proportion, it's because Michelangelo designed it to be seen "correctly" from far below the rooftop of the church.)

The colossus was placed standing up in a cart and dragged across rollers from Michelangelo's workshop (behind the Duomo) to the Palazzo Vecchio, where the statue replaced a work by Donatello. There *David* stood—naked and outdoors—for 350 years. In the right light, you can see signs of weathering on his shoulders. Also, note the crack in *David*'s left arm where it was broken off during a 1527 riot near the Palazzo Vecchio. In 1873, to conserve the masterpiece, the statue was finally replaced with a copy (✪ see photo below) and moved here. The real *David* now stands under a wonderful Renaissance-style dome designed just for him.

Circle *David* and view him from various angles. From the front, he's confident, but a little less so when you gaze directly into his eyes. Around

His oversized right hand, powered by God

David once guarded the Town Hall entrance.

back, see his sling strap, buns of steel, and Renaissance mullet. Up close, you can see the blue-veined Carrara marble and a few cracks and stains. From the sides, Michelangelo's challenge becomes clear: to sculpt a figure from a block of marble other sculptors said was too tall and narrow to accommodate a human figure.

Renaissance Florentines could identify with *David*. Like him, they considered themselves God-blessed underdogs fighting their city-state rivals. In a deeper sense, they were civilized Renaissance people slaying the ugly giant of medieval superstition, pessimism, and oppression.

▶ *Hang around for a while. Eavesdrop on tour guides. The Plexiglas shields at the base of the statue went up after an attack by a frustrated artist, who smashed the statue's feet in 1991.*

Lining the hall leading up to David *are other statues by Michelangelo—his* Prisoners, St. Matthew, *and* Pietà. *Start with the* Awakening Prisoner, *the statue at the end of the nave (farthest from* David). *He's on your left as you face* David.

The *Prisoners* (*Prigioni*, c. 1516-1534)

These unfinished figures seem to be fighting to free themselves from the stone. Michelangelo believed the sculptor was a tool of God, not creating but simply revealing the powerful and beautiful figures that God had encased in the marble. Michelangelo's job was to chip away the excess, to reveal. He needed to be in tune with God's will, and whenever the spirit came upon him, Michelangelo worked in a frenzy, without sleep, often for days on end.

The *Prisoners* give us a glimpse of this fitful process, showing the restless energy of someone possessed, struggling against the rock that binds him. Michelangelo himself fought to create the image he saw in his mind's eye. You can still see the grooves from the chisel, and you can picture Michelangelo hacking away in a cloud of dust. Unlike most sculptors, who built a model and then marked up their block of marble to know where to chip, Michelangelo always worked freehand, starting from the front and working back. These figures emerged from the stone (as his colleague Vasari put it) "as though surfacing from a pool of water."

The so-called **Awakening Prisoner** (the names were given by scholars, not Michelangelo) seems to be stretching after a long nap, still tangled in his "bedsheets" of uncarved rock. He's more block than statue.

More Michelangelo

If you're a fan of earth's greatest sculptor, you won't leave Florence until there's a check next to each of these:

- **Bargello:** Several Michelangelo sculptures, including the *Bacchus* (pictured here; see the Bargello Tour chapter).
- **Duomo Museum:** Another moving *Pietà* (see page 96 of the Duomo Museum Tour chapter).
- **Medici Chapels:** The *Night* and *Day* statues, plus others done for the Medici tomb, located at the Basilica of San Lorenzo (see page 119).
- **Laurentian Library:** Michelangelo designed the entrance staircase and more, located at the Basilica of San Lorenzo (see page 118).
- **Palazzo Vecchio:** His *Victory* statue (see page 114).
- **Uffizi Gallery:** A rare Michelangelo painting (see page 68 of the Uffizi Gallery Tour chapter).
- **Casa Buonarroti:** Built on property Michelangelo once owned, at Via Ghibellina 70, containing some early works (see page 123).
- **Santa Croce Church:** Michelangelo's tomb (see page 122).
- **Santo Spirito Church:** Wooden crucifix thought to be by Michelangelo (see page 132).

On the right, the **Young Prisoner** is more finished. He buries his face in his forearm, while his other arm is chained behind him.

The *Prisoners* were designed for the never-completed tomb of Pope Julius II (who also commissioned the Sistine Chapel ceiling). Michelangelo may have abandoned them simply because the project itself petered out, or he may have deliberately left them unfinished. Having perhaps satisfied himself that he'd accomplished what he set out to do, and seeing no

Unfinished *Prisoner* fights to free himself.

Powerful *Pietà,* possibly by Michelangelo

point in polishing them into their shiny, finished state, he went on to a new project.

Walking up the nave toward David, you'll pass by Michelangelo's **St. Matthew** (1503), on the right. Though not one of the Prisoners series, he is also unfinished, perfectly illustrating Vasari's "surfacing" description.

The next statue (also on the right), the **Bearded Prisoner,** is the most finished of the four, with all four limbs, a bushy face, and even a hint of daylight between his arm and body.

Across the nave on the left, the **Atlas Prisoner** carries the unfinished marble on his stooped shoulders, his head still encased in the block.

As you study the *Prisoners,* notice Michelangelo's love and understanding of the human body. His greatest days were spent sketching the muscular, tanned, and sweating bodies of the workers in the Carrara marble quarries. The prisoners' heads and faces are the least-developed part—they "speak" with their poses. Comparing the restless, claustrophobic *Prisoners* with the serene and confident *David* gives an idea of the sheer emotional range in Michelangelo's work.

Pietà

In the unfinished *Pietà* (the threesome closest to *David*), the figures struggle to hold up the sagging body of Christ. Michelangelo (or, more likely, one of his followers) emphasizes the heaviness of Jesus' dead body, driving home the point that this divine being suffered a very human death. Christ's massive arm is almost the size of his bent and broken legs. By stretching his body—if he stood up, he'd be more than seven feet tall—the weight is exaggerated.

▶ *After getting your fill of Michelangelo, consider taking a spin around the rest of the Accademia. Michelangelo's statues are far and away the highlight here, but the rest of this small museum—housed in a former convent/hospice—has a few bonuses.*

Paintings

Browse the pleasant-but-underwhelming collection of paintings in the hall near David and the adjoining corridor; you'll be hard-pressed to find even one by a painter whose name you recognize. You'll find better art in the Giambologna Room near the exit (described below.)

Salone dell'Ottocento Statues

At the end of the hall to the left of *David* is a long room crammed with plaster statues and busts. These were the Academy art students' "final exams"—preparatory models for statues, many of which were later executed in marble. The black dots on the statues are sculptors' "points," guiding them on how deep to chisel. The Academy art school has been attached to the museum for centuries, and you may see the next Michelangelo wandering the streets nearby.

Bust of Michelangelo by Daniele da Volterra

At the end of the nave (farthest from *David*), a bronze bust depicts a craggy, wrinkled Michelangelo, age 89, by Daniele da Volterra. (Daniele, one of Michelangelo's colleagues and friends, is best known as the one who painted loincloths on the private parts of Michelangelo's nudes in the Sistine Chapel.) As a teenager, Michelangelo got his nose broken in a fight with a rival artist. Though Michelangelo went on to create great beauty, he was never classically handsome.

▶ *Enter the room near the museum entrance dominated by a large, squirming statue.*

Giambologna Room—*The Rape of the Sabine Women* (1582)

This full-size plaster model guided Giambologna's assistants in completing the marble version in the Loggia dei Lanzi (on Piazza della Signoria, next to the Palazzo Vecchio, ✪ described on page 32). A Roman warrior tramples a fighter from the Sabine tribe and carries off the man's wife. Husband and wife exchange one final, anguished glance. Circle the statue and watch it spiral to life around its axis.

Giambologna was clearly influenced (as a plaque with photo points out) by Michelangelo's groundbreaking *Victory* in the Palazzo Vecchio (1533-1534). Michelangelo's statue of a man triumphing over a fallen enemy introduced both the theme and the spiral-shaped pose that many artists imitated.

The room also contains minor **paintings** by artists you'll encounter elsewhere in Florence. There are works by Botticelli, whose *Birth of Venus* hangs in the Uffizi (✪ see page 62). Filippino Lippi is known for his frescoes in the Brancacci Chapel and Church of Santa Maria Novella. Domenico Ghirlandaio's paintings of Renaissance Florence are behind the altar of the Church of Santa Maria Novella (✪ see page 124). Benozzo Gozzoli decorated the personal chapel of the Medici in the Medici-Riccardi Palace (✪ see page 121). And Francesco Granacci, a childhood friend of Michelangelo, assisted him on the Sistine Ceiling.

▶ *From the Giambologna Room, head down a short hallway leading to a few rooms containing the...*

Museum of Musical Instruments

Between 1400 and 1700, Florence was one of Europe's most sophisticated cities, and the Medici rulers were trendsetters. Musicians like Scarlatti and Handel flocked to the court of Prince Ferdinando (1663-1713). You'll see late-Renaissance cellos, dulcimers, violins, woodwinds, and harpsichords. (Listen to some on the computer terminals.)

As you enter, look for the two group paintings that include the prince (he's second from the right in both paintings, with the yellow bowtie) hanging out with his musician friends. The gay prince played a mean harpsichord, and he helped pioneer new variations. In the adjoining room, you'll see several experimental keyboards, including some by Florence's keyboard pioneer, Bartolomeo Cristofori. The tall piano on display (from 1739) is considered by some to be the world's first upright piano.

▶ *Head one more time back up the nave to say goodbye to Dave, then turn left, and left again, to go through the bookstore toward the exit. Before you leave—after the bookshop, but before the exit lobby—you'll see stairs up to the first floor, with one more exhibit. At the top is...*

Painting in Florence (Pittura a Firenze) 1370-1430

Here you'll find mostly altarpieces depicting saints and Madonnas, painted during the last gasp of the Middle Ages—the period after the Great Plague wracked Florence, but before Renaissance fever hit in full force.

Gaze upon Lorenzo Monaco's *Man of Sorrows* (up the stairs, in the central hall, 1404), and mentally contrast this somber scene with the confident optimism of Michelangelo's *David,* done a century later, in the full bloom of the Florentine Renaissance.

▶ *The tour is finished. From here, it's a 10-minute walk to the Duomo.*

Uffizi Gallery Tour

Galleria degli Uffizi

In the Renaissance, Florentine artists rediscovered the beauty of the natural world. Medieval art had been symbolic, telling Bible stories. Realism didn't matter. But Renaissance people saw the beauty of God in nature and the human body. They used math and science to capture the natural world on canvas as realistically as possible.

The Uffizi Gallery (oo-FEED-zee) has the greatest overall collection anywhere of Italian painting. We'll trace the rise of realism and savor the optimistic spirit that marked the Renaissance. As Michelangelo wrote:

My eyes love things that are fair,
and my soul for salvation cries.
But neither will to Heaven rise
unless the sight of Beauty lifts them there.

ORIENTATION

Cost: €12.50 (or €8 if there's no temporary exhibit), additional €4 fee for recommended reservation, free and crowded on the first Sun of the month, covered by Firenze Card.

Hours: Tue-Sun 8:15-18:35, closed Mon.

Reservations: To avoid the notoriously long ticket-buying lines (up to 3 hours April-Oct; an hour in Nov-March), either get a Firenze Card or make reservations. For details on both, ✪ see page 169. For April-Oct and weekends, reserve a month or more in advance. Off-season, you can sometimes just walk right in without a reservation late in the day. The most crowded days are Tue, Sat, and Sun.

Getting There: It's on the Arno River by the Palazzo Vecchio.

Getting In: There are several entrances (see map on page 54).

Door #1 (labeled *Reservation Entrance*), is for those with a Firenze Card or a reserved ticket already in hand. (To actually claim your reserved ticket, you must first go to door #3, see below.)

Door #2 is to buy tickets (without a reservation). This door also sells same-day reservations and Firenze Cards.

Door #3 (labeled *Reservation Ticket Office*) is the first stop for those who've made reservations but need to pick up their tickets. Arrive 10 minutes before your appointed time. If you booked online (paying with a credit card), show your voucher to get a ticket. If you or your hotelier booked by phone, show your confirmation number and pay for the ticket. Once you have your ticket, walk across the courtyard to Door #1 and enter.

Information: Tel. 055-238-8651, reservation tel. 055-294-883, www. uffizi.firenze.it.

Tours: A 1.5-hour audioguide costs €6 (€10/2 people; must leave ID). ✪ Download my free Uffizi Gallery **audio tour.**

Length of This Tour: Allow two hours.

Cloakroom: Baggage check is available in the entrance lobby. No bottled liquids allowed.

Services: In the entrance/exit hall (once past security), there's a book/gift shop (with nice cheap guidebooks and art-themed souvenirs), a post office, and WCs in the basement (find stairs near the cloakroom). Once in the gallery, there are no WCs until near the end of our tour, on the staircase leading down from the café.

Botticelli's *Venus*—for lovers of beauty

Crowded Uffizi entrance—plan ahead

Photography: No flash photography.

Cuisine Art: The café at the end of the top-floor gallery has a simple indoors area with pricey sandwiches, salads, desserts, and fruit cups (cash only). If you pay more to sit outside on the terrace, you're treated to stunning views of the Palazzo Vecchio and the Duomo's dome. A €5 cappuccino with that view is one of Europe's great treats.

Starring: Botticelli, Venus, Raphael, Giotto, Titian, Leonardo, and Michelangelo.

THE TOUR BEGINS

The Ascent

▶ *Walk up the four long flights of the monumental staircase to the top floor (those with limited mobility can take the elevator). Your brain should be fully aerated from the hike up.*

At the top of the stairs, just before the ticket taker, stop to survey the busts of the Medici family. Once you're past the ticket taker, get oriented.

OVERVIEW

The Uffizi is U-shaped, running around the courtyard. Most of the collection is on this one floor, displayed chronologically. This left wing focuses on Florentine art from medieval to Renaissance times. At the far end, you pass through a short hallway filled with sculpture. The right wing (which you can see across the courtyard) has later Florentine art (especially Michelangelo) and a café terrace facing the Duomo. The visit continues downstairs

Uffizi Gallery Overview

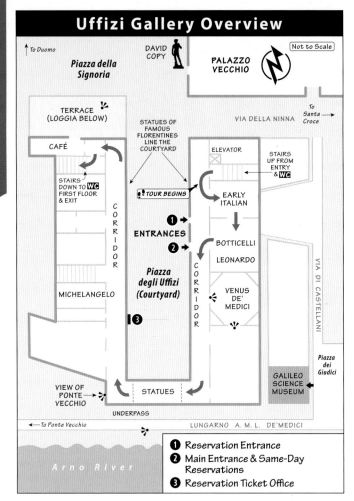

Not to Scale

To Duomo

Piazza della Signoria

DAVID COPY

PALAZZO VECCHIO

TERRACE (LOGGIA BELOW)

CAFÉ

STATUES OF FAMOUS FLORENTINES LINE THE COURTYARD

VIA DELLA NINNA

To Santa Croce

ELEVATOR

STAIRS UP FROM ENTRY & **WC**

STAIRS DOWN TO **WC** FIRST FLOOR & EXIT

TOUR BEGINS

EARLY ITALIAN

CORRIDOR

❶ ➡ **ENTRANCES**

❷ ➡

BOTTICELLI

LEONARDO

VIA DI CASTELLANI

Piazza degli Uffizi (Courtyard)

CORRIDOR

VENUS DE' MEDICI

MICHELANGELO

❸

Piazza dei Giudici

GALILEO SCIENCE MUSEUM

VIEW OF PONTE VECCHIO

STATUES

UNDERPASS

To Ponte Vecchio

LUNGARNO A. M. L. DE'MEDICI

Arno River

❶ Reservation Entrance

❷ Main Entrance & Same-Day Reservations

❸ Reservation Ticket Office

with many more rooms of art, showing how the Florentine Renaissance spread to Rome (Raphael) and Venice (Titian), and inspired the Baroque (Caravaggio). We'll concentrate on the Uffizi's forte, the Florentine section, then get a taste of the art that followed.

▶ *Head up the long hallway, and enter the first door on the left.*

Medieval—When Art Was as Flat as the World (1200-1400)

Duccio, Cimabue, and Giotto—A Trio of Madonnas with Child

In this room, three pre-Renaissance paintings show the slow process of learning to paint a 3-D world on a 2-D surface. In each work, Mary and Baby Jesus sit on a throne in a golden never-never land symbolizing heaven. It's as if medieval Christians couldn't imagine holy people inhabiting our dreary material world. It took Renaissance painters to bring Mary down to earth and give her human realism. For the Florentines, "realism" meant "three-dimensional."

The similar-looking Madonna-and-Bambinos in this room—all painted within a few decades of each other in about the year 1300—show baby steps in the march to realism. **Duccio**'s piece (on the left as you face Giotto) is the most medieval and two-dimensional. There's no background. The angels are just stacked one on top of the other, floating in the golden atmosphere. Mary's throne is crudely drawn—the left side is at a

Duccio's *Madonna*—a cardboard cutout; Cimabue—more substantial; Giotto—massive Mary on 3-D throne

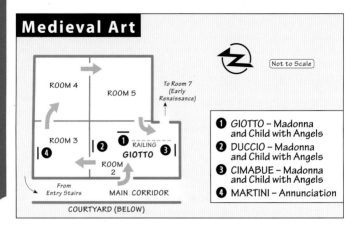

Medieval Art

ROOM 4

ROOM 5

To Room 7
(Early
Renaissance)

Not to Scale

ROOM 3

RAILING

GIOTTO

ROOM 2

From
Entry Stairs

MAIN CORRIDOR

COURTYARD (BELOW)

❶ GIOTTO – Madonna
and Child with Angels

❷ DUCCIO – Madonna
and Child with Angels

❸ CIMABUE – Madonna
and Child with Angels

❹ MARTINI – Annunciation

three-quarter angle while the right is practically straight on. Mary herself is a wispy cardboard-cutout figure seemingly floating just above the throne.

On the opposite wall, the work of **Cimabue**—mixing the iconic Byzantine style with budding Italian realism—is an improvement. The large throne creates an illusion of depth; the angels alongside peek out from behind its massive architecture. Mary's foot actually sticks out over the lip of the throne. Still, the angels are stacked totem-pole-style, serving as heavenly bookends. Cimabue wowed the people of his day with his technique (including his much-loved crucifix for the Church of Santa Croce; see page 122), but he was quickly overshadowed by one of his students—Giotto—who grew to be more talented and famous.

Giotto employs realism to make his theological points. He creates a space and fills it. Like a set designer, he builds a three-dimensional "stage"—the canopied throne—then peoples it with real beings. The throne has angels in front, prophets behind, and a canopy over the top, clearly defining its three dimensions. The steps up to the throne lead from our space to Mary's, making the scene an extension of our world. But the real triumph here is Mary herself—big and monumental, like a Roman statue. Beneath her robe, she has a real live body, with knees and breasts that stick out at us. This three-dimensionality was revolutionary in its day, a taste of the Renaissance a century before it began.

Giotto was one of the first "famous" artists. In the Middle Ages, artists

Annunciation—saints in golden Neverland

Adoration—exquisite detail, cramped 3-D

were mostly unglamorous craftsmen, like carpenters or cable-TV repair-men. They cranked out generic art and could have signed their work with a bar code. But Giotto was recognized as a genius, a unique individual. He died in a plague that devastated Florence. If there had been no plague, would the Renaissance have started 100 years earlier?

▶ *Enter Room 3 featuring art from Siena. It's to the left as you face Giotto.*

Simone Martini (c. 1284-1344)—*Annunciation*

Simone Martini boils things down to the basic figures needed to get the message across: (1) The angel appears to sternly tell (2) Mary that she'll be the mother of Jesus. In the center is (3) a vase of lilies, a symbol of purity. Above is (4) the Holy Spirit as a dove about to descend on her. If the sym-bols aren't enough to get the message across, Simone Martini has spelled it right out for us in Latin: *"Ave Gratia Plena..."* or, "Hail, favored one, the Lord is with you." Mary doesn't exactly look pleased as punch.

This is not a three-dimensional work. The point was not to re-create reality but to teach religion, especially to the illiterate masses. This isn't a beautiful Mary or even a real Mary. She's a generic woman without distinc-tive features. We know she's pure—not from her face, but only because of the halo and symbolic flowers. Before the Renaissance, artists didn't care about the beauty of individual people.

Simone Martini's *Annunciation* has medieval features you'll see in many of the paintings in the next few rooms: (1) religious subject, (2) gold background, (3) two-dimensionality, and (4) meticulous detail.

▶ *Pass through Rooms 4 and 5, full of golden altarpieces. Exiting Room 5, hang a U-turn left into Room 7.*

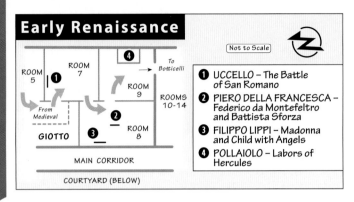

Early Renaissance

Not to Scale

ROOM 5 • ❶
ROOM 7
❹ → To Botticelli
ROOM 9
ROOMS 10-14
From Medieval
❷
GIOTTO ❸ ROOM 8

MAIN CORRIDOR

COURTYARD (BELOW)

❶ UCCELLO – The Battle of San Romano

❷ PIERO DELLA FRANCESCA – Federico da Montefeltro and Battista Sforza

❸ FILIPPO LIPPI – Madonna and Child with Angels

❹ POLLAIOLO – Labors of Hercules

Gentile da Fabriano (c. 1370-1427)—*Adoration of the Magi*

Look at the incredible detail of the Three Kings' costumes, the fine horses, and the cow in the cave. The canvas is filled from top to bottom with realistic details—but it's far from realistic. While the Magi worship Jesus in the foreground, their return trip home dangles over their heads in the "background."

This is a textbook example of the International Gothic style popular with Europe's aristocrats in the early 1400s: well-dressed, elegant people in a colorful, design-oriented setting. The religious subject is just an excuse to paint secular luxuries such as jewelry and clothes made of silk brocade. And the scene's background and foreground are compressed together to create an overall design that's pleasing to the eye. Such exquisite detail work raises the question: Was Renaissance three-dimensionality truly an improvement over Gothic, or simply a different style?

Early Renaissance (mid-1400s)

▶ *Enter Room 8. In the center of the room stands a double portrait.*

Piero della Francesca (c. 1412-1492)—*Federico da Montefeltro and Battista Sforza*

In medieval times, only saints and angels were worthy of being painted. In the humanistic Renaissance, however, even nonreligious folk like this husband and wife had their features preserved for posterity. Usually the man would have appeared on the left, with his wife at the right. But Federico's

Warts-and-all celebration of a real man

Beautiful *Madonna* radiates holiness.

right side was definitely not his best—he lost his right eye and part of his nose in a tournament. Renaissance artists discovered the beauty in ordinary people and painted them, literally, warts and all.

Fra Filippo Lippi (1406-1469)—*Madonna and Child with Two Angels*

Compare this Mary with the generic female in Simone Martini's *Annunciation*. We don't need the wispy halo over her head to tell us she's holy—she radiates sweetness and light from her divine face. Heavenly beauty is expressed by a physically beautiful woman.

Fra (Brother) Lippi, an orphan raised as a monk, lived a less-than-monkish life. He lived with a nun who bore him two children. He spent his entire life searching for the perfect Virgin. Through his studio passed Florence's prettiest girls, many of whom decorate the walls here in this room.

Lippi painted idealized beauty, but his models were real flesh-and-blood human beings. You could look through all the thousands of paintings from the Middle Ages and not find anything so human as the mischievous face of one of Lippi's little angel boys.

▶ *Enter Room 9, with two tiny works by Pollaiolo in the glass case between the windows.*

Antonio del Pollaiolo (c. 1431-1498)—*Labors of Hercules*

Hercules gets a workout in two small panels showing the human form at odd angles. The poses are the wildest imaginable, to show how each muscle twists and tightens. While Uccello worked on perspective, Pollaiolo studied anatomy. In medieval times, dissection of corpses was a sin and a crime (the two were the same then). Dissecting was a desecration of the

Pollaiolo dissected corpses to learn how to depict realistic musculature in extreme poses.

human body, the temple of God. But Pollaiolo was willing to sell his soul to the devil for artistic knowledge. He dissected.

There's something funny about this room that I can't put my finger on...I've got it—no Madonnas. Not one. (No, that's not a Madonna; she's a Virtue.)

We've seen how Early Renaissance artists worked to conquer reality. Now let's see the fruits of their work, the flowering of Florence's Renaissance.

▶ *Enter the large Botticelli room and take it all in. (If room is under renovation, paintings are in Room 41.)*

Florence—The Renaissance Blossoms (1450-1500)

Florence in 1450 was in a Firenz-y of activity. There was a can-do spirit of optimism in the air, led by prosperous merchants and bankers and a strong middle class. The government was reasonably democratic, and Florentines saw themselves as citizens of a strong republic—like ancient Rome. Their civic pride showed in the public monuments and artworks

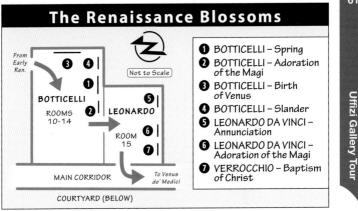

The Renaissance Blossoms

From Early Ren.

Not to Scale

BOTTICELLI
ROOMS 10-14

LEONARDO

ROOM 15

MAIN CORRIDOR

To Venus de' Medici

COURTYARD (BELOW)

❶ BOTTICELLI – Spring
❷ BOTTICELLI – Adoration of the Magi
❸ BOTTICELLI – Birth of Venus
❹ BOTTICELLI – Slander
❺ LEONARDO DA VINCI – Annunciation
❻ LEONARDO DA VINCI – Adoration of the Magi
❼ VERROCCHIO – Baptism of Christ

they built. Man was leaving the protection of the church to stand on his own two feet.

Lorenzo de' Medici, head of the powerful Medici family, epitomized this new humanistic spirit. Strong, decisive, handsome, poetic, athletic, sensitive, charismatic, intelligent, brave, clean, and reverent, Lorenzo was a true Renaissance Man, deserving of the nickname he went by—the Magnificent. He gathered Florence's best and brightest around him for evening wine and discussions of great ideas. One of this circle was the painter Botticelli.

Sandro Botticelli (1445-1510)—*Spring*

It's springtime in a citrus grove. The winds of spring blow in (Mr. Blue, at right), causing the woman on the right to sprout flowers from her lips as she morphs into Flora, or Spring—who walks by, spreading flowers from her dress. At the left are Mercury and the Three Graces, dancing a delicate maypole dance. The Graces may be symbolic of the three forms of love—love of beauty, love of people, and sexual love, suggested by the raised intertwined fingers. (They forgot love of peanut butter on toast.) In the center stands Venus, the Greek goddess of love. Above her flies a blindfolded Cupid, happily shooting his arrows of love without worrying whom they'll hit.

Here is the Renaissance in its first bloom, its "springtime" of innocence. Madonna is out, Venus is in. Adam and Eve hiding their nakedness

Botticelli's *Primavera* captures the springtime of the Renaissance, showing gods on earth.

are out, glorious flesh is in. This is a return to the pre-Christian pagan world of classical Greece, where things of the flesh are not sinful. But this is certainly no orgy—just fresh-faced innocence and playfulness.

Botticelli emphasizes pristine beauty over gritty realism. The lines of the bodies, especially of the Graces in their see-through nighties, have pleasing, S-like curves. The faces are idealized but have real human features. There's a look of thoughtfulness and even melancholy in the faces— as though everyone knows that the innocence of spring will not last forever.

▶ *Look at the next painting to the right.*

Botticelli—*Adoration of the Magi*
Here's the rat pack of confident young Florentines who reveled in the optimistic pagan spirit—even in a religious scene. Botticelli included himself among the adorers, at the far right, looking vain in the yellow robe. Lorenzo is the Magnificent-looking guy at the far left.

Botticelli—*Birth of Venus*
According to myth, Venus was born from the foam of a wave. Still only half awake, this fragile, newborn beauty floats ashore on a clamshell, blown

The Greek Goddess of Love slowly awakens after a thousand years of medieval darkness.

by the winds, where her maid waits to dress her. The pose is the same S-curve of classical statues (as we'll soon see). Botticelli's pastel colors make the world itself seem fresh and newly born.

This is the purest expression of Renaissance beauty. Venus' naked body is not sensual, but innocent. Botticelli thought that physical beauty was a way of appreciating God. Remember Michelangelo's poem: Souls will never ascend to heaven "...unless the sight of Beauty lifts them there."

Botticelli finds God in the details—Venus' windblown hair, her translucent skin, the maid's braided hair, the slight ripple of the wind god's abs, and the flowers tumbling in the slowest of slow motions, suspended like musical notes, caught at the peak of their brief life.

Mr. and Mrs. Wind intertwine—notice her hands clasped around his body. Their hair, wings, and robes mingle like the wind. But what happened to those splayed toes?

▶ *"Venus on the Half-Shell" (as many tourists call this) is one of the masterpieces of Western art. Take some time with it. Then find the small canvas on the wall to the right, near* Spring.

Botticelli—*Slander* (a.k.a. *Calumny of Apelles*)
The spring of Florence's Renaissance had to end. Lorenzo died young.

The economy faltered. Into town rode the monk Savonarola, preaching medieval hellfire and damnation for those who embraced the "pagan" Renaissance spirit. "Down, down with all gold and decoration," he roared. "Down where the body is food for the worms." He presided over huge bonfires, where the people threw in their fine clothes, jewelry, pagan books... and paintings.

Slander spells the end of the Florentine Renaissance. The architectural setting is classic Brunelleschi, but look what's taking place beneath those stately arches. These aren't proud Renaissance men and women but a ragtag, medieval-looking bunch, a Court of Thieves in an abandoned hall of justice. The accusations fly, and everyone is condemned. The naked man pleads for mercy, but the hooded black figure, a symbol of his execution, turns away. The figure of Truth (naked Truth)—straight out of *The Birth of Venus*—looks up to heaven as if to ask, "What has happened to us?" The classical statues in their niches look on in disbelief.

Botticelli got caught up in the teachings of Savonarola. He burned some of his own paintings and changed his artistic tune. The last works of his life were darker, more somber, and pessimistic about humanity.

The 19th-century German poet Heinrich Heine said, "When they start by burning books, they'll end by burning people." After four short years of power, Savonarola was burned in 1498 on his own bonfire in Piazza della Signoria, but by then the city was in shambles. The first flowering of the Renaissance was over.

▶ *Enter the next room (#15).*

Leonardo da Vinci (1452-1519)—*Annunciation*

A scientist, architect, engineer, musician, and painter, Leonardo was a true Renaissance man. He worked at his own pace rather than to please an employer, so he often left works unfinished. The two paintings in this room aren't his best, but even a lesser Leonardo is enough to put a museum on the map, and they're definitely worth a look.

In the *Annunciation,* the angel Gabriel has walked up to Mary, and now kneels on one knee like an ambassador, saluting her. See how relaxed his other hand is, draped over his knee. Mary, who's been reading, looks up with a gesture of surprise and curiosity.

Leonardo constructs a beautifully landscaped "stage" and puts his characters in it. Look at the bricks on the right wall. If you extended lines from them, the lines would all converge at the center of the painting, the

Botticelli's *Slander*—chaos reigns   Leonardo's *Annunciation*—underlying order

distant blue mountain. Same with the edge of the sarcophagus and the railing. This subtle touch creates a subconscious feeling of balance, order, and spaciousness in the viewer.

Think back to Simone Martini's *Annunciation* to realize how much more natural, relaxed, and realistic Leonardo's version is. He's taken a miraculous event—an angel appearing out of the blue—and presented it in a very human way.

Leonardo da Vinci—*Adoration of the Magi*
Leonardo's human insight is even more apparent here, in this unfinished work (it may be under restoration during your visit). The poor kings are amazed at the Christ child—even afraid of him. They scurry around like chimps around a fire. This work is as agitated as the *Annunciation* is calm, giving us an idea of Leonardo's range. Leonardo was pioneering a new era of painting, showing not just outer features but the inner personality.

The next painting to the right, *Baptism of Christ,* is by Andrea del Verrocchio, Leonardo's teacher. Leonardo painted the angel on the far left when he was only a teenager. Legend has it that when Verrocchio saw that some kid had painted an angel better than he ever would...he hung up his brush for good.

Florence saw the first blossoming of the Renaissance. But when the cultural climate turned chilly, artists flew south to warmer climes. The Renaissance shifted to Rome.

▶ *Proceed past the Leonardo into the small hallway. Straight ahead is a doorway (with a glass barrier) to the Tribuna (a.k.a. Room 18). Gazing inside, you'll see the famous* Venus de' Medici *statue.*

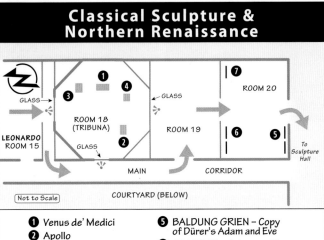

Classical Sculpture & Northern Renaissance

ROOM 20

ROOM 18 (TRIBUNA)

ROOM 19

LEONARDO ROOM 15

GLASS

MAIN   CORRIDOR

Not to Scale   COURTYARD (BELOW)

To Sculpture Hall

❶ Venus de' Medici
❷ Apollo
❸ The Wrestlers
❹ The Knife Grinder
❺ BALDUNG GRIEN – Copy of Dürer's Adam and Eve
❻ CRANACH – Adam and Eve
❼ CRANACH – Martin Luther and Katherina von Bora

Tribune Room

If the Renaissance was the foundation of the modern world, the foundation of the Renaissance was classical sculpture. Sculptors, painters, and poets alike turned for inspiration to these ancient Greek and Roman works as the epitome of balance, 3-D perspective, human anatomy, and beauty.

Venus de' Medici, first century B.C.

Is this pose familiar? Botticelli's *Birth of Venus* has the same position of the arms, the same S-curved body, and the same lifting of the right leg. A copy of this statue stood in Lorenzo the Magnificent's garden, where Botticelli used to hang out. This one is a Roman copy of the lost original by the great Greek sculptor Praxiteles. Balanced, harmonious, and serene, the statue embodies the attributes of Greece's "Golden Age," when balance was admired in every aspect of life.

Perhaps more than any other work of art, this statue *(Venere dei Medici)* has been the epitome of both ideal beauty and sexuality. In the

18th and 19th centuries, sex was "dirty," so the sex drive of cultured aristo-crats was channeled into a love of pure beauty. Wealthy sons and daughters of Europe's aristocrats made the pilgrimage to the Uffizi to complete their classical education...where they swooned in ecstasy before the cold beauty of this goddess of love.

Louis XIV had a bronze copy made. Napoleon stole her away to Paris for himself. And in Philadelphia in the 1800s, a copy had to be kept under lock and key to prevent the innocent from catching the Venere-al disease. At first, it may be difficult for us to appreciate such passionate love of art, but if any generation knows the power of sex to sell something—be it art or underarm deodorant—it's ours.

The Other Statues, first-second century A.D.

The male counterpart to *Venus de' Medici* faces her from across the room. *Apollo* (a.k.a. "Venus with a Penis") is another Greco-Roman interpretation of the master of smooth, cool lines: Praxiteles.

The other works are later Greek (Hellenistic), when quiet balance was replaced by violent motion and emotion. *The Wrestlers,* to the left of Venus, is a study in anatomy and twisted limbs—like Pollaiolo's paintings a thousand years later.

The drama of *The Knife Grinder* to the right of Venus stems from the off-stage action—he's sharpening the knife to flay a man alive.

This fine room was a showroom, or a "cabinet of wonders," back when this building still functioned as the Medici offices. Filled with family portraits, it's a holistic statement that symbolically links the Medici family with the four basic elements: air (weathervane in the lantern), water (inlaid mother of pearl in the dome), fire (red wall), and earth (inlaid stone floor).

▶ *Exit into the main hallway. Breathe. Sit. Admire the ceiling. Look out the window. See you in five.*

Back already? Now continue down the hallway. At the end of the hall, turn right and stroll through the...

Sculpture Hall

A hundred years ago, no one even looked at Botticelli—they came to the Uffizi to see the sculpture collection. And today, these 2,000-year-old Roman copies of 2,500-year-old Greek originals are hardly noticed...but they should be. Only a few are displayed here now.

The most impressive is the male nude, **Doriforo** ("spear carrier").

Scholars have long suspected that this statue, a Roman marble copy of a Greek bronze original, once carried a lance in his left hand as he strolled along.

The purple statue in the center of the hall—headless and limbless—is a **female wolf** (*lupa*, c. A.D. 120) done in porphyry stone. This was the animal that raised Rome's legendary founders and became the city's symbol. Renaissance Florentines marveled at the ancient Romans' ability to create such lifelike, three-dimensional works. They learned to reproduce them in stone...and then learned to paint them on a two-dimensional surface.

▶ *Gaze out the windows from the hall. At the far end, enjoy the best...*

View of the Arno and the Ponte Vecchio

Enjoy Florence's best view of the river and Ponte Vecchio. You can also see the red-tiled roof of the Vasari Corridor, the "secret" passage connecting the Palazzo Vecchio, Uffizi, Ponte Vecchio, and the Pitti Palace on the other side of the river—a half-mile in all. This was a private walkway, wall-papered in great art, for the Medici family's commute from home to work.

As you appreciate the view (best at sunset), remember that it's this sort of pleasure that Renaissance painters wanted you to get from their paintings. For them, a canvas was a window you looked through to see the wide world. Their paintings re-create natural perspective: Distant objects (such as bridges) are smaller, dimmer, and higher up the "canvas," while closer objects are bigger, clearer, and lower.

We're headed down the home stretch now. If your little U-feetsies are killing you, and it feels like torture, remind yourself that it's a pleasant torture, and smile...like the statue next to you.

▶ *Round the bend and start down the far hallway. A few steps along, turn left into Room 35 and head for the round painting opposite the entry.*

Michelangelo Room

Michelangelo Buonarroti (1475-1564)—*Holy Family*, a.k.a. *Doni Tondo*

This is the only completed easel painting by the greatest sculptor in history. Florentine painters were sculptors with brushes; this shows it. Instead of a painting, it's more like three clusters of statues with some clothes painted on.

The main subject is the holy family—Mary, Joseph, and Baby Jesus—and in the background are two groups of nudes looking like classical

Michelangelo's *Holy Family*—earthy

Raphael's *Madonna*—graceful and balanced

statues. The background represents the old pagan world, while Jesus in the foreground is the new age of Christianity. The figure of young John the Baptist at right is the link between the two.

This is a "peasant" Mary, with a plain face and sunburned arms. Michelangelo shows her from a very unflattering angle—we're looking up her nostrils. But Michelangelo himself was an ugly man, and he was among the first artists to recognize the beauty in everyday people.

Michelangelo was a Florentine—in fact, he was like an adopted son of the Medici, who recognized his talent—but much of his greatest work was done in Rome as part of the pope's face-lift of the city. We can see here some of the techniques he used on the Sistine Chapel ceiling that revolutionized painting—monumental figures; dramatic angles (looking up Mary's nose); accentuated, rippling muscles; and bright, clashing colors (all the more apparent since both this work and the Sistine Chapel ceiling have recently been cleaned). These elements added a dramatic tension that was lacking in the graceful work of Leonardo and Botticelli.

Michelangelo painted this for his friend Agnolo Doni for 70 ducats. (Michelangelo designed, but didn't carve, the elaborate frame.) When the painting was delivered, Doni tried to talk Michelangelo down to 40. Proud Michelangelo took the painting away and would not sell it until the man finally agreed to pay double...140 ducats.

Also on display in the room is the hard-to-miss statue of **Sleeping Ariadne.** The third-century work was much copied, and Michelangelo was inspired by it. (Hmm. Does Mary in the *Doni Tondo* have a few touches of Ariadne? The twisting pose, the position of the arms, and the heavily wrinkled robe?)

▶ *Continue down the hallway—past the special exhibits and rooms where masterpieces from closed rooms are temporarily displayed.*

Laocoön (16th-century copy)

At the far end of the hall is a copy of the dramatic ancient Greek statue of Laocoön (the original is at the Vatican Museums). One of the most famous statues of antiquity, it was discovered in 1506—just in time to inspire Renaissance greats like Michelangelo. But right now Mr. Laocoön says, "Time for a coffee break." Just past him is a fine café and an open-air terrace where you can enjoy a truly aesthetic experience...

▶ *The staircase just past Room 35 leads to the exit. But before you leave, consider browsing...*

The Rest of the Uffizi

The final rooms on the top floor contain Mannerist and Baroque art, as artists took Renaissance realism and exaggerated it still more—more beauty, more emotion, more drama. The staircase near Room 35 leads to some WCs, the temporary exhibits, the Caravaggio Rooms (starring *The Sacrifice of Isaac*), and the exit.

Or, before heading down, just relax at the top-floor café, enjoying a cappuccino on the view terrace. This drinkable art form is called the "Little Capuchin Monk" because the coffee's frothy light- and dark-brown foam looks like the two-toned cowls of the Capuchin order. Sip it in the shadow of the towering Palazzo Vecchio, and be glad we live in an age where you don't need to be a Medici to enjoy all this fine art. *Salute.*

When you're ready to move on, the modern-looking staircase near the café takes you past the WC down to the ground floor where you will find two Rembrandt self-portraits (in Room 49).

▶ *As you make your way to the exit, definitely stop in Room 66 for...*

Raphael (Raffaello Sanzio, 1483-1520)—*Madonna of the Goldfinch*

Raphael brings Mary and bambino down from heaven and into the real world of trees, water, and sky. He gives Baby Jesus (right) and John the Baptist a realistic, human playfulness. It's a tender scene painted with warm colors and a hazy background that matches the golden skin of the children.

Raphael perfected his craft in Florence, following the graceful style of Leonardo. In typical Leonardo fashion, this group of Mary, John the Baptist, and Jesus is arranged in the shape of a pyramid, with Mary's head at the peak.

The two halves of the painting balance perfectly. Draw a line down the middle, through Mary's nose and down through her knee. John the Baptist on the left is balanced by Jesus on the right. Even the trees in the background balance each other, left and right. These things aren't immediately noticeable, but they help create the subconscious feelings of balance and order that reinforce the atmosphere of maternal security in this domestic scene—pure Renaissance.

Raphael—*Leo X and Cardinals*

Raphael was called to Rome at the same time as Michelangelo, working next door in the Vatican apartments while Michelangelo painted the Sistine Chapel ceiling. Raphael peeked in from time to time, learning from Michelangelo's monumental, dramatic figures, and his later work is grittier and more realistic than the idealized, graceful, and "Leonardoesque" Madonna.

Pope Leo X is big, like a Michelangelo statue. And Raphael captures some of the seamier side of Vatican life in the cardinals' eyes—shrewd, suspicious, and somewhat cynical. With Raphael, the photographic realism pursued by painters since Giotto was finally achieved.

The Florentine Renaissance ended in 1520 with the death of Raphael. Raphael (see his **self-portrait** nearby) is considered both the culmination and conclusion of the Renaissance. The realism, balance, and humanism we associate with the Renaissance are all found in Raphael's work. He combined the grace of Leonardo with the power of Michelangelo. With his death, the Renaissance shifted again—to Venice.

▸ *A few rooms farther along, you reach Room 74, with a tall painting by...*

Six Degrees of Leo X

This sophisticated, luxury-loving pope was at the center of an international Renaissance world that spread across Europe. He crossed paths with many of the Renaissance men of his generation. Based on the theory that any two people are linked by only "six degrees of separation," let's link Leo X with the actor Kevin Bacon:

- Leo X's father was Lorenzo the Magnificent, patron of Botticelli and Leonardo.
- When Leo X was age 13, his family took in 13-year-old Michelangelo.
- Michelangelo inspired Raphael, who was later hired by Leo X.
- Raphael exchanged masterpieces with fellow genius Albrecht Dürer, who was personally converted by Martin Luther (who was friends with Lucas Cranach), who was excommunicated by...Leo X.
- Leo X was portrayed in the movie *The Agony and the Ecstasy*, which starred Charlton Heston, who was in *Planet of the Apes* with Burgess Meredith, who was in *Rocky* with Sylvester Stallone, who was in *Cop Land* with Robert De Niro, who was in *Sleepers* with...Kevin Bacon.

Parmigianino (1503-1540)—*Madonna with the Long Neck*

Once Renaissance artists had mastered reality, where could they go next?

Mannerists such as Parmigianino tried, by going beyond realism, exaggerating it for effect. Using brighter colors and twisting poses, they created scenes more elegant and more exciting than real life.

By stretching the neck of his Madonna, Parmigianino (like the cheese) gives her an unnatural, swanlike beauty. She has the same pose and position of hands as Botticelli's *Venus* and the *Venus de' Medici*. Her body forms an arcing S-curve—down her neck as far as her elbow, then back the other way along Jesus' body to her knee, then down to her foot. Baby

Jesus seems to be blissfully gliding down this slippery slide of sheer beauty.

▶ *Continue on to long Room 83, with a number of works by...*

Titian (c. 1490-1576)—*Venus of Urbino*

Compare this Venus with Botticelli's newly hatched Venus, and you get a good idea of the difference between the Florentine and Venetian Renaissance. Botticelli's was pure, innocent, and otherworldly. Titian's should have a staple in her belly button. This isn't a Venus, it's a centerfold—with no purpose but to please the eye (and other organs). While Botticelli's allegorical Venus is a message, this is a massage. The bed is used.

Titian and his fellow Venetians took the pagan spirit pioneered in Florence and carried it to its logical hedonistic conclusion. Using bright, rich colors, they captured the luxurious life of happy-go-lucky Venice.

While other artists may have balanced their compositions with a figure on the left and one on the right, Titian balances his painting in a different way—with color. The canvas is split down the middle by the curtain. The left half is dark, the right half is lighter. The two halves are connected by a diagonal slash of luminous gold—the nude woman. The girl in the background is trying to find her some clothes.

In the Uffizi, we've seen many images of female beauty: from ancient goddesses to medieval Madonnas, from Parmigianino's cheesy slippery-slide to Michelangelo's peasant Mary, from Botticelli's pristine nymphs to Titian's sensuous centerfold. Their physical beauty expresses different aspects of the human spirit.

By the way, visitors from centuries past reportedly panted in front of this Venus by Titian. The Romantic poet Byron called it "*the* Venus." With her sensual skin, hey-sailor look, and suggestively placed hand, she must have left them blithering idiots.

▶ *Our tour is n-n-n-nearly over. Turn left through a long connecting hallway, then left again into still more rooms. It's worth pausing in Room 90, with works by Caravaggio, including the shocking ultrarealism of* The Sacrifice of Isaac.

When you're ready to leave, the exit takes you back down to the WCs/bookstore/post office, and the way out to the street. You'll pop out behind the Uffizi, a block up from the river and very near the Galileo Science Museum and the Bargello (sculpture museum).

Bargello Tour

The Renaissance began with sculpture. The great Florentine painters were "sculptors with brushes." You can see the birth of this revolution of 3-D in the Bargello (bar-JEL-oh), which boasts the best collection of Florentine sculpture.

You'll see Donatello's *David,* a sly little boy who slew a giant. The museum has the original contest panels for the Baptistery doors, the event that kicked off the Renaissance. And there are several Michelangelo statues—less-famous works that show off different aspects of his varied style.

The Bargello is relatively small and uncrowded, a pleasant break from the intensity of the rest of city. After enduring the intensity of the Uffizi, take a quiet stroll through the Bargello, and immerse yourself in the ambience of Renaissance Florence.

ORIENTATION

Cost: €7 (or €4 if no special exhibits), cash only, free and crowded on first Sun of the month, covered by Firenze Card.

Hours: Tue-Sat 8:15-17:00, until 13:50 if there are no special exhibits; also open second and fourth Mon and first, third, and fifth Sun of each month. You can reserve an entrance time, but it's unnecessary. Tel. 055-238-8606, www.polomuseale.firenze.it.

Getting There: Via del Proconsolo 4, a two-minute walk northeast of the Palazzo Vecchio.

Getting In: You must pass through a metal detector to enter. No liquids are allowed in the museum.

Tours: Audioguide rentals are €6 (€10/2 people).

Length of This Tour: Allow one hour.

With Limited Time: See the Michelangelo room on the ground floor and the Donatello room on the first floor.

Photography: Permitted without flash.

Starring: Michelangelo, Donatello, Brunelleschi, Ghiberti, and four different *David*s.

THE TOUR BEGINS

Courtyard

▶ *Buy your ticket and take a seat in the courtyard.*

The Bargello, built in 1255, was once Florence's original Town Hall and also served as a police station *(bargello)*, and later a prison. The heavy

fortifications tell us that keeping the peace in medieval Florence had its occupational hazards.

The Bargello, a three-story rectangular building, surrounds this cool and peaceful courtyard. The best statues are found in two rooms—one on the ground floor at the foot of the outdoor staircase, and another one flight up, directly above. We'll proceed from Michelangelo to Donatello to Verrocchio.

But first, meander around this courtyard and get a feel for sculpture in general and the medium of stone in particular. Sculpture is a much more robust art form than painting. Think of just the engineering problems of the sculpting process: quarrying and cutting the stone, transporting the block to the artist's studio, all the hours of chiseling away chips, then the painstaking process of sanding the final product by hand. A sculptor must be strong enough to gouge into the stone, but delicate enough to groove out the smallest details. Think of Michelangelo's approach to sculpting: He wasn't creating a figure—he was liberating it from the rock that surrounded it.

The Renaissance was centered on humanism—and sculpture is the perfect medium in which to express it. It shows the human form, standing alone, independent of church, state, or society, ready to create itself.

Finally, a viewing tip. Every sculpture has an invisible "frame" around it—the stone block it was cut from. Visualizing this frame helps you find the center of the composition.

Ground Floor

▶ *Head into the room at the foot of the courtyard's grand staircase. Enter, turn left, and watch for a party animal on the right.*

Michelangelo—*Bacchus,* c. 1497

Bacchus, the god of wine and revelry, raises another cup to his lips, while his little companion goes straight for the grapes.

Maybe Michelangelo had a sense of humor after all. Mentally compare this tipsy Greek god of wine with his sturdy, sober *David,* begun a few years later. Raucous *Bacchus* isn't nearly so muscular, so monumental... or so sure on his feet. Hope he's not driving. The pose, the smooth muscles, the beer belly, and the swaying hips look more like Donatello's boyish *David.*

This was Michelangelo's first major commission. He often vacillated between showing man as strong and noble, or as weak and perverse. This isn't the nobility of the classical world, but the decadent side of orgies and indulgence.

▶ *Just beyond* Bacchus *is...*

Michelangelo—*Brutus,* 1540

Another example of the influence of Donatello is this so-ugly-he's-beautiful bust by Michelangelo. His rough intensity gives him the look of a man who has succeeded against all odds, a dignified and heroic quality that would be missing if he were too pretty.

The subject is Brutus, the Roman who, for the love of liberty, murdered his friend and dictator, Julius Caesar *("Et tu...?").* Michelangelo could understand this man's dilemma. He himself was torn between his love of the democratic tradition of Florence and loyalty to his friends the Medici, who had become dictators.

So he gives us two sides of a political assassin. The right profile (the

Another side to Michelangelo besides *David:* *Bacchus* (left) is debauched, while *Brutus* broods

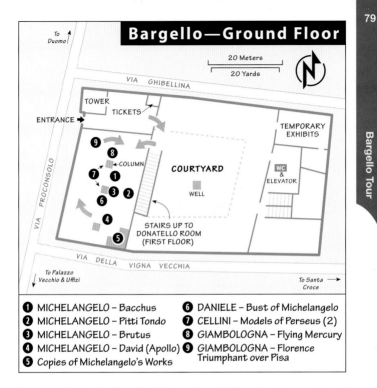

Bargello—Ground Floor

To Duomo

20 Meters
20 Yards

VIA GHIBELLINA

TOWER
ENTRANCE ➤
TICKETS

VIA PROCONSOLO

COLUMN

COURTYARD

WELL

TEMPORARY
EXHIBITS

WC &
ELEVATOR

STAIRS UP TO
DONATELLO ROOM
(FIRST FLOOR)

VIA DELLA VIGNA VECCHIA

To Palazzo
Vecchio & Uffizi

To Santa
Croce

❶ MICHELANGELO – Bacchus
❷ MICHELANGELO – Pitti Tondo
❸ MICHELANGELO – Brutus
❹ MICHELANGELO – David (Apollo)
❺ Copies of Michelangelo's Works

❻ DANIELE – Bust of Michelangelo
❼ CELLINI – Models of Perseus (2)
❽ GIAMBOLOGNA – Flying Mercury
❾ GIAMBOLOGNA – Florence
Triumphant over Pisa

front view) is heroic. But the hidden side, with the drooping mouth and squinting eye, makes him more cunning, sneering, and ominous.

▸ *Also nearby is...*

Michelangelo–*David* a.k.a. *Apollo,* 1530-1532

This restless, twisting man is either David or Apollo. (Is he reaching for a sling or a quiver?) Demure (and left unfinished), this statue is light years away from Michelangelo's famous *David* in the Accademia, which is so much larger than life in every way. We'll see three more *Davids* upstairs. As you check out each one, compare and contrast the artists' styles.

In the glass cases in the corner are small-scale copies of some of

Donatello (1386-1466)

Donatello was the first great Renaissance genius, a model for Michelangelo and others. He mastered realism, creating the first truly lifelike statues of people since ancient times. Donatello's work is highly personal. Unlike the ancient Greeks—but like the ancient Romans—he often sculpted real people, not idealized versions of pretty gods and goddesses. Some of these people are downright ugly. In the true spirit of Renaissance humanism, Donatello appreciated the beauty of flesh-and-blood human beings.

Donatello's personality was also a model for later artists. He was moody and irascible, purposely setting himself apart from others in order to concentrate on his sculpting. He developed the role of the "mad genius" that Michelangelo would later perfect.

Michelangelo's most famous works. In this area, also look for a bust of Michelangelo by his fellow sculptor Daniele da Volterra, capturing his broken nose and brooding nature. (You may recognize this bust from the Accademia, which has a copy.)

▶ Doubling back toward the entrance, you'll find...

Cellini—Models of Perseus, 1545-1554
The life-size statue of Perseus slaying Medusa, located in the open-air loggia next to the Palazzo Vecchio, is cast bronze. Benvenuto Cellini started with these smaller models (one in wax, one in bronze) to get the difficult process down. When it came time to cast the full-size work, everything was going fine...until he realized he didn't have enough metal! He ran around the studio, gathering up pewterware and throwing it in, narrowly avoiding a mess-terpiece.

Giambologna—Flying Mercury, before 1580
Catch this statue while you can—he's in a hurry to deliver those flowers. Despite all the bustle and motion, Mercury has a solid Renaissance core: the line of balance that runs straight up the center, from toes to hip to fingertip. He's caught in midstride. His top half leans forward, counterbalanced

by his right leg in back, while the center of gravity rests firmly at the hip-bone. Down at the toes, notice the cupid practicing for the circus.

Giambologna—*Florence Triumphant over Pisa*, c. 1575-1580

This sculpture shows the fierce Florentine chauvinism that was born in an era when Italy's cities struggled for economic and political dominance... and Florence won.

▶ *To see the roots of Florence's Renaissance, climb the courtyard staircase to the next floor up and turn right into the large Donatello room.*

First Floor

▶ *Entering the room, cross to the middle of the far wall, and check out the first of three Davids in this room (the one wearing the long skirt).*

Donatello—An early *David*, c. 1408

This is young Donatello's first take on the popular subject of David slaying Goliath. His dainty pose makes him a little unsteady on his feet. He's dressed like a medieval knight (fully clothed but showing some leg through the slit skirt). The generic face and blank, vacant eyes give him the look not of a real man but of an anonymous decoration on a church facade. At age 22, Donatello still had one foot in the old Gothic style. To tell the story of David, Donatello plants a huge rock right in the middle of Goliath's forehead.

▶ *From here, circle the room clockwise. The next statue is the same subject, by a different artist.*

Andrea del Verrocchio—*David*, c. 1466-1469

Verrocchio (1435-1488) is best known as the teacher of Leonardo da Vinci, but he was also the premier sculptor of the generation between Donatello and Michelangelo. Verrocchio's *David* is definitely the shepherd "boy" described in the Bible. (Some have speculated that the statue was modeled on Verrocchio's young, handsome, curly-haired apprentice, Leonardo da Vinci.) David leans on one leg, not with a firm, commanding stance but a nimble one (especially noticeable from behind). Compare the smug smile of the victor with Goliath's "Oh, have I got a headache" expression.

▶ *Finally, near the corner, is...*

Bargello—First Floor

To Duomo

20 Meters

20 Yards

VIA GHIBELLINA

TOWER

VIA PROCONSOLO

CHAPEL

DONATELLO ROOM

COURTYARD

ELEVATOR

STAIRS UP FROM GROUND FLOOR

STAIRS UP TO SECOND FLOOR

UPPER LOGGIA

VIA DELLA VIGNA VECCHIA

To Palazzo Vecchio & Uffizi

To Santa Croce

1 DONATELLO – David (c. 1408)

2 VERROCCHIO – David (c. 1469)

3 DONATELLO – David (c. 1440)

4 DESIDERIO – Niccolò da Uzzano

5 DONATELLO – St. George

6 DESIDERIO – St. John the Baptist

7 GHIBERTI & BRUNELLESCHI – The Sacrifice of Isaac (2 versions)

8 DELLA ROBBIA – Relief Panels

Donatello—*David*, c. 1440

He's naked. Donatello sees David as a teenage boy wearing only a helmet, boots, and sword (this sculpture is often cited by scholars who think the artist was homosexual). The smooth-skinned warrior sways gracefully, poking his sword playfully at the severed head of the giant Goliath. His *contrapposto* stance is similar to Michelangelo's *David,* resting his weight on one leg in the classical style, but it gives him a feminine rather than masculine look. Gazing into his coy eyes and at his bulging belly is a very different experience from confronting Michelangelo's older and sturdier Renaissance Man.

This *David* paved the way for Michelangelo's. Europe hadn't seen a freestanding male nude like this in a thousand years. In the Middle Ages, the human body was considered a dirty thing, a symbol of man's weakness, something to be covered up in shame. The church prohibited exhibitions of nudity like this one and certainly would never decorate a church with it. But in the Renaissance, a new class of rich and powerful merchants appeared, and they bought art for personal enjoyment. Reading Plato's *Symposium,* they saw the ideal of Beauty in the form of a young man. This particular statue stood in the palace of the Medici (today's Medici-Riccardi Palace)... where Michelangelo, practically an adopted son, grew up admiring it.

Verrocchio's *David*—small but confident

Donatello's *David*—coy, sensuous, and nude

Now's a good time to compare the four different *David*s that we've seen. Verrocchio's saucy, impertinent *David* has more attitude than Donatello's generic warrior, and is younger and more masculine than Donatello's girlish, gloating *David*. He's more vigorous than Michelangelo's unfinished *David/Apollo* but he's a far cry from Michelangelo's monumental version.

▶ *Along the wall behind the last* David *is...*

Desiderio da Settignano—*Niccolò da Uzzano*, after 1450

Not an emperor, not a king, not a pope, saint, or prince, this is one of Florence's leading businessmen in a toga, portrayed in the style of an ancient Roman bust. In the 1400s, when Florence was inventing the Renaissance that all Europe would soon follow, there was an optimistic spirit of democracy that gloried in everyday people. Desiderio, one of Donatello's best students, portrayed this man as he was—with wrinkles, a quizzical look, and bags under his eyes.

▶ *In the niche just above and to the right of* Uzzano, *you'll see...*

An ordinary businessman shown heroically   Donatello's *St. George* inspired Florentines.

Donatello—*St. George*, c. 1417

The proud warrior has both feet planted firmly on the ground and stands on the edge of his niche looking out alertly. He tenses his powerful right hand as he prepares to attack. George, the Christian slayer of dragons, was just the sort of righteous warrior proud Renaissance Florentines could rally around in their struggles with nearby cities. Nearly a century later, Michelangelo's *David* replaced *George* as the unofficial symbol of Florence, but *David* was clearly inspired by *George*'s relaxed intensity and determination. (This is the original statue; a copy stands in its original niche at Orsanmichele Church— ✪ see page 28.)

The relief panel below shows George doing what he's been pondering. To his right, the sketchy arches and trees create the illusion of a distant landscape. Donatello, who apprenticed in Ghiberti's studio, is credited with teaching his master how to create 3-D illusions like this.

▶ St. John the Baptist, *begun by Donatello and finished by his student, is to the right.*

Desiderio da Settignano (and Donatello)—*St. John the Baptist*, c. 1450-1455

John the Baptist was the wild-eyed, wildcat prophet who lived in the desert preaching, living on bugs 'n' honey, and baptizing Saviors of the world. Donatello, the mad prophet of the coming Renaissance, might have identified with this original eccentric.

▶ *On the wall next to* George, *you'll find some bronze relief panels. Don't look at the labels just yet.*

Ghiberti and Brunelleschi—Baptistery Door Competition Entries, 1401

Some would say these two different relief panels (pictured on the next page) represent the first works of the Renaissance. These two versions of *The Sacrifice of Isaac* were finalists in a contest held in 1401 to decide who would create the bronze doors of the Baptistery. The contest sparked citywide excitement, which evolved into the Renaissance spirit. Lorenzo Ghiberti won and later did the doors known as the Gates of Paradise. Filippo Brunelleschi lost—fortunately for us—freeing him to design the Duomo's dome.

Both artists catch the crucial moment when Abraham, obeying God's orders, prepares to slaughter and burn his only son as a sacrifice. At the

Ghiberti's, on the left, won.

last moment—after Abraham has passed this test of faith—an angel of God appears to stop the bloodshed.

Let's look at the composition of the two panels: One is integrated and cohesive (yet dynamic), while the other is a balanced knickknack shelf of segments. Human drama: One has bodies and faces that speak. The boy's body is a fine classical nude in itself, so real and vulnerable. Abraham's face is intense and ready to follow God's will. Perspective: An angel zooms in from out of nowhere to save the boy in the nick of time.

Is one panel clearly better than the other? You be the judge. Pictured below are the two finalists for the Baptistery door competition—Ghiberti's and Brunelleschi's. Which do you like better?

It was obviously a tough call, but Ghiberti's was chosen, perhaps because his goldsmith training made him better suited for the technical end.

▶ *Back near the room's entrance, you'll find several colorful terra-cotta reliefs.*

Luca della Robbia—Terra-Cotta Relief Panels

Mary and baby Jesus with accompanying angels look their most serene in these panels by the master of painted, glazed porcelain. Polished blue, white, green, and yellow, they have a gentle and feminine look that softens the rough masculine stone of this room. Luca was just one of a family of Della Robbias who pioneered art in terra-cotta.

The Rest of the Bargello

The museum is filled with objects that reflect life in Renaissance Florence. Other first-floor rooms display ivories, jewelry, and Renaissance dinnerware. Fans of Italian majolica should visit Room 6. The easy-to-miss second floor (find the carpeted staircase marked *Al 2° Piano*) has Della Robbia terra-cotta panels and miniature bronze models of famous statues.

From swords to statues, from *Brutus* to Brunelleschi, from *David* to *David* to *David* to *David*—the Bargello's collection of civilized artifacts makes it clear why Florence dominated the Italian Renaissance.

Duomo Museum Tour

Museo dell'Opera del Duomo

Brunelleschi's dome, Ghiberti's bronze doors, and Donatello's statues—these creations define the 1400s (the Quattrocento) in Florence, when the city blossomed and classical arts were reborn. All are featured at the Duomo Museum, plus a Michelangelo *Pietà* that was intended as his sculptural epitaph. While copies decorate the exteriors of the Duomo (cathedral), Baptistery, and Campanile (bell tower, called Giotto's Tower), the original sculptured masterpieces of the complex are restored and fill the Duomo Museum.

ORIENTATION

Changes Likely: The museum has just reopened after a major remodel. At the time of this printing, this was our best guess at the details. Expect a few changes.

Cost: €15 combo-ticket covers all Duomo sights; also covered by Firenze Card.

Hours: Daily 9:00-19:00, last entry one hour before closing. This is one of the few museums in Florence that is always open on Monday.

Getting There: The museum is behind the Duomo (its east end), at Via del Proconsolo 9.

Information: Tel. 055-282-226 or 055-230-7885, www.operaduomo.firenze.it.

Tours: The audioguide costs €5. Guided English tours are generally offered daily in summer for €3 (times vary).

Length of This Tour: Allow 1.5 hours.

With Limited Time: Focus on Ghiberti's doors, Michelangelo's *Pietà*, Donatello's sculptures, and Brunelleschi's dome model.

Photography: Allowed, but no flash around paintings.

THE TOUR BEGINS

The Duomo Museum tells the history of the Duomo: constructed in the 14th century, topped with a dome in the 15th century, decorated with sculpture by generations of artists, and finally finished in the 19th century with a colorful facade.

GROUND FLOOR

Model of the Duomo's Medieval Facade

▶ *Browse the first few small rooms.*

The Duomo began life as a humble church alongside the more prestigious Baptistery. By the 1200s, the church wasn't big enough to contain the exuberant spirit of a city growing rich from the wool trade and banking. In 1296, the cornerstone was laid for a huge church—today's Duomo— intended to be the biggest in Christendom.

Arnolfo di Cambio, the architect, designed the facade. It was under construction for nearly three centuries (1296-1587) and never completed. Only the bottom third was ever covered with marble facing—the upper part remained bare brick. Had Arnolfo's design been completed, the three-story facade would have looked much like today's colorful, Neo-Gothic version, with pointed arches and white, pink, and green marble, studded with statues and gleaming with gold mosaics. In 1587, the still incomplete facade was torn down. The model suggests the glory of Arnolfo's original vision.

▶ *A hundred years later, Arnolfo's medieval facade became a showcase for Renaissance sculptors. The museum has some 40 of those statues. Focus on some of the key statues that sat in niches on the facade.*

Facade Statues

Madonna with the Glass Eyes (Madonna in Trono col Bambino)

Arnolfo personally designed this cheery statue to sit directly above the main doorway, welcoming visitors. The building was dedicated to Mary— starry-eyed over the birth of baby Jesus. She sits, crowned like a chess-set queen, framed with a dazzling mosaic halo. She was accompanied (to our right) by St. Zenobius, Florence's first bishop during Roman times, whose raised hand consecrated the formerly pagan ground as Christian.

Statue of Pope Boniface VIII

Despised by Dante for his meddling in politics, this pope paid 3,000 florins to get his image in a box seat high on the upper left of the facade. His XL shirt size made him look correct when viewed from below. Though the statue

Two statues from the Duomo's original facade: *Madonna* over the door, and a straight-backed pope

is stylized, Arnolfo realistically shows the pope's custom-made, extra-tall hat and bony face. (Most of the room's statues are straight-backed, to hang on the facade.)

Donatello—*St. John the Evangelist (San Giovanni Evangelista)*

A hundred years later, Arnolfo's medieval facade became a showcase for Renaissance sculptors.

John sits gazing at a distant horizon, his tall head rising high above his massive body. This visionary foresees a new age...and the coming Renaissance. The right hand is massive—as relaxed as though it were dangling over the back of a chair, but full of powerful tension. Like the mighty right hand of Michelangelo's *David,* and the beard of Michelangelo's *Moses,* this work is a hundred years ahead of its time.

At 22 years old, Donatello (c. 1386-1466) sculpted this work just before becoming a celebrity for his inspiring statue of *St. George* (original in the Bargello, copy on the exterior of the Orsanmichele Church). Donatello ("Little Donato"), like most early Renaissance artists, was a blue-collar worker, raised as a workshop apprentice among knuckle-dragging musclemen. He proudly combined physical skill with technical know-how to create beauty (Art + Science = Renaissance Beauty). His statues are thinkers with big hands who can put theory into practice.

▶ *Opposite the model of the facade stand the famous bronze doors by Lorenzo Ghiberti.*

Ghiberti's Baptistery Doors

The Renaissance began in 1401 with a citywide competition to build new doors for the Baptistery. Lorenzo Ghiberti (c. 1378-1455) won the job and built the doors for the north side of the building. Everyone loved them, so he was then hired to make another set of doors—these panels—for the main entrance facing the Duomo. These bronze "Gates of Paradise" (1425-1452) revolutionized the way Renaissance people saw the world around them.

The original 10 panels from the Gates of Paradise were moved from the Baptistery to the museum to better preserve them. Copies now adorn the Baptistery itself. (✪ See the graphic on page 23 for the original layout.) The panels are under glass to protect against natural light, and gassed with nitrogen to guard them against oxygen and humidity.

Ghiberti, the illegitimate son of a goldsmith, labored all his working life (more than 50 years) on the two Baptistery doors. Their execution was a major manufacturing job, requiring a large workshop of artists and artisans for each stage of the process: making the door frames that hold the panels, designing and making models of the panels (forming them in wax in order to cast them in bronze), gilding the panels (by bathing them in powdered gold dissolved in mercury, then heating until the gold and bronze blended), polishing the panels, mounting them, installing the doors...and signing paychecks for everyone along the way. Ghiberti was as much businessman as artist.

▶ *Here's a description of a few of the panels:*

Joseph and Benjamin (Storie di Giuseppe e Beniamino)

With just the depth of a thumbnail, Ghiberti creates a temple in the round inhabited by workers. This round temple wowed Florence. Armed with the rules of perspective, Ghiberti rendered reality with a mathematical precision we don't normally impose on what we see, when our eyes and minds settle for ballpark estimates about relative size and distance. For Florentines, suddenly the world acquired a whole new dimension—depth.

The Creation of Adam and Eve (La Creazione e Storie di Adamo ed Eva)

Ghiberti tells several stories in one panel—a common medieval technique—by using different thicknesses in the relief. In the sketchy background (very low relief), God in a bubble conducts the Creation. In the center (a little thicker), Eve springs from Adam's side. Finally, in the lower

Ghiberti's Baptistery door panels: *Joseph and Benjamin* (left) and *The Creation of Adam and Eve*

left (in high relief), an elegantly robed God pulls Adam, as naked as the day he was born, from the mud.

Ghiberti welcomed the innovations of other artists. See the angel flying through an arch (right side). This arch is in very low relief but still looks fully 3-D because it's rendered sideways, using the perspective tricks of painting. Ghiberti learned the technique from one of his employees, the young Donatello.

Jacob and Esau (Storie di Giacobbe ed Esau)
The "background" arches and the space they create are as interesting as the scenes themselves. At the center is the so-called vanishing point on the distant horizon, where all the arches and floor tiles converge. This calm center gives us an eye-level reference point for all the figures. Those closest to us, at the bottom of the panel, are big and clearly defined. Distant figures are smaller, fuzzier, and higher up.

Ghiberti has placed us about 20 feet away from the scene, part of this casual crowd of holy people—some with their backs to us—milling around an arcade.

Labors of Adam, and Cain and Abel
(Il Lavoro dei Progenitori e Storie di Caino e Abele)
On one mountain, we see Cain and Abel offering a sacrifice at the top, Adam waving at the bottom, and the first murder in between. In early panels such as this, Ghiberti used only a sketchy landscape as a backdrop for human activities.

Cain and Abel—a mountainside murder

Solomon and Sheba—all eyes go toward them

Solomon and the Queen of Sheba (Salomone e la Regina di Saba)
The receding arches stretch into infinity, giving the airy feeling that we can see forever. All of the arches and steps converge at the center of the panel, where the two monarchs meet, uniting their respective peoples. Ghiberti's subject was likely influenced by the warm ecumenical breeze blowing through Florence in 1439, as religious leaders convened here in an attempt to reunite the eastern (Constantinople) and western (Rome) realms of Christendom.

If the Renaissance began in 1401 with Ghiberti's doors, it ended in 1555 with Michelangelo's *Pietà* (which we'll see soon).

▶ *Displayed near the famous Gates of Paradise you'll find…*

Other Baptistery Artifacts
The **Roman sarcophagi** found near here remind us that Florence's religious history stretches back to ancient times. The Baptistery (11th century) was likely built on the site of a pagan Roman temple.

Flanking Ghiberti's famous bronze doors are his nearly-as-famous **North Doors.** These are the doors Ghiberti made for the 1401 competition that kicked off the Renaissance. Though they dazzled people at the time with their 3-D realism, they're most noteworthy today to illustrate how much further Ghiberti took the concept with the Gates of Paradise 25 years later.

Spiritual Statues
Also on the ground floor are rooms dedicated to the museum's most famous and evocative statues.

Florence's history dates back to the Romans.

Magdalene's rippling hair suggests turmoil.

Donatello—*Mary Magdalene* (*Maddalena,* c. 1455)

Carved from white poplar and originally painted with realistic colors, this statue is less a Renaissance work of beauty than a medieval object of intense devotion.

Mary Magdalene—the prostitute rescued from the streets by Jesus—folds her hands in humble prayer. Her once-beautiful face and body have been scarred by fasting, repentance, and the fires of her own remorse. The matted hair sticks to her face; veins and tendons line the emaciated arms and neck. The rippling hair suggests emotional turmoil within. But from her hollow, tired eyes, a new beauty shines, an enlightened soul that doesn't rely on the external beauty of human flesh.

The man who helped rebirth the classical style now shocked Florence by turning his back on it. Picking up a knife, he experimented in the difficult medium of woodcarving, where subtlety can get lost when the wood splits off in larger-than-wanted slivers.

Sixty-five-year-old Donatello had just returned to Florence, after years away. His city had changed. Friends were dying (Brunelleschi died before they could reconcile after a bitter fight), favorite pubs were overrun with frat boys, and Florence was gaga over Greek gods in pretty, gleaming marble. Donatello fell into a five-year funk, completing only two statues, including this one.

Michelangelo—*Pietà* (1547-1555)

The aging Michelangelo (1475-1564) designed his own tomb, with this as the centerpiece. He was depressed by old age, the recent death of his soul mate, and the grim reality that by sculpting this statue he was writing his

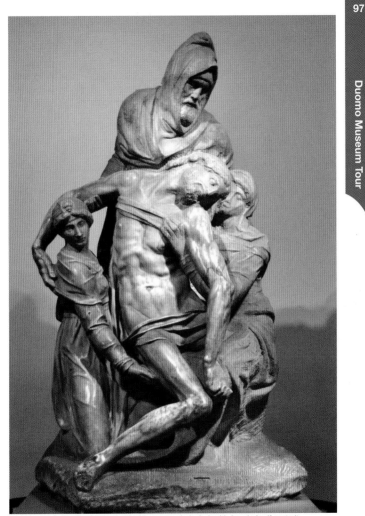

Michelangelo's late *Pietá,* intended for his own tomb, includes his hooded self-portrait.

own obituary. Done on his own dime, it's fair to consider this an introspective and very personal work.

Three mourners tend the broken body of the crucified Christ. We see Mary, his mother (the shadowy figure on our right); Mary Magdalene (on the left, polished up by a pupil); and Nicodemus, the converted Pharisee, whose face is clearly that of Michelangelo himself. The polished body of Christ stands out from the unfinished background. Michelangelo (as Nicodemus), who spent a lifetime bringing statues to life by "freeing" them from the stone, looks down at what could be his final creation, the once-perfect body of Renaissance Man that is now twisted, disfigured, and dead.

Seen face-on, the four figures form a powerful geometric shape of a circle inside a triangle, split down the middle by Christ's massive (but very dead) arm. Seen from the right side, they seem to interact with each other, their sketchy faces changing emotions from grief to melancholy to peaceful acceptance.

Fifty years earlier, a confident Michelangelo had worked here on these very premises, skillfully carving *David* from an imperfect block. But he hated this marble for the *Pietà;* it was hard and grainy, and gave off sparks when hit wrong. (The chisel grooves in the base remind us of the sheer physical effort of a senior citizen sculpting.) Worst of all, his housekeeper kept bugging him with the same question that Pope Julius II used to ask about the Sistine Chapel—"When will you finish?" Pushed to the edge, Michelangelo grabbed a hammer and attacked the flawed marble statue, hacking away and breaking off limbs, then turned to the servant and said, "There! It's finished!" (An assistant later repaired some of the damage, but cracks are still visible in Christ's left arm and only leg.)

▶ *Continue upstairs to the first floor, to a large room lined with two stone balconies.*

FIRST FLOOR

Room of the Cantorie

This room displays two marble choir lofts *(cantorie)* that once sat above the sacristy doors of the Duomo.

Luca della Robbia—*Cantoria* (1430-c. 1438)

After almost 150 years of construction, the cathedral was nearly done, and the Opera del Duomo, the workshop in charge, began preparing the interior for the celebration. Brunelleschi hired a little-known sculptor, 30-year-old Luca della Robbia, to make this *cantoria,* a balcony choir box for singers in the cathedral. It sums up the exuberance of the Quattrocento. The panels are a celebration of music, song, and dance performed by toddlers, children, and teenagers.

The *cantoria* brings Psalm 150 to life like a YouTube video. Starting in the upper left, the banner reads *"Laudate D.N.M."*—"Praise the Lord"—while children laugh and dance to the sound of trumpets *("sono Tubae")* and guitars, autoharps, and tambourines *("Psaltero… Cythera… Timpano")*. In the next level down, kids dance ring-around-the-rosy, a scene in the round on an almost-flat surface, showing front, back, and in-between poses. At bottom right, the Psalm ends: "Everybody praise the Lord!" Della Robbia's choir box was a triumph, a celebration of Florence's youthful boom time.

The Della Robbia family is best known for their colorful glazed terracotta, some of which you'll likely see in the Duomo Museum and around town.

Donatello—*Cantoria* (1433-c. 1440)

If Della Robbia's balcony looks like afternoon recess, Donatello's looks like an all-night rave. Donatello's figures are sketchier, murky, and frenetic, as the dancing kids hurl themselves around the balcony. Imagine candles lighting this as they seem to come to life. If the dance feels almost pagan, there's a reason.

Recently returned from a trip to Rome, Donatello carved in the style of

Choir boxes from the original church: Della Robbia's (left) is exuberant, Donatello's is dark

classical friezes of dancing *putti* (chubby, playful toddlers). This choir box stood in a dark area of the Duomo, so Donatello chose colorful mosaics and marbles to catch the eye, while purposely leaving the dancers unfinished and shadowy, tangled figures flitting inside the columns. In the dim light, worshippers swore they saw them move.

▶ Find the gallery with statues and panels that once decorated the Campanile.

Gallery of Campanile Decorations

The Duomo's bell tower, designed by Giotto and augmented by Arnolfo di Cambio, also served as a colorful sculpture gallery. The museum has the original 16 statues (by several sculptors) from the bell tower's third story, where copies stand today.

Donatello did several statues of the prophets, plus some others with collaborators. (Some statues may be under restoration during your visit.)

Donatello invented the Renaissance style that Michelangelo would later perfect—powerful statues that are ultra-realistic, even ugly, sculpted in an "unfinished" style by an artist known for experimentation and his prickly, brooding personality. Both men were famous but lived like peasants, married only to their work.

Donatello—*Habakkuk (Abacuc)*

Donatello's signature piece shows us the wiry man beneath the heavy mantle of a prophet. Habakkuk's rumpled cloak falls down the front, dividing the body lengthwise. From the deep furrows emerges a bare arm with well-defined tendons and that powerful right hand. His long, muscled

Donatello's eccentric prophet *Habakkuk*

Jeremiah smolders as Jerusalem burns.

neck leads to a bald head (the Italians call the statue *Lo Zuccone,* meaning "pumpkin head").

The ugly face, with several days' growth of beard, crossed eyes, and tongue-tied mouth, looks crazed. This is no confident Charlton Heston prophet, but a man who's spent too much time alone, fasting in the wilderness, searching for his calling, and who now returns to babble his vision on a street corner.

Donatello, the eccentric prophet of a new style, identified with this statue, talking to it, swearing at it, yelling at it: "Speak!"

▶ *Nearby, look for...*

Donatello—*Jeremiah (Geremia)*

Watching Jerusalem burn in the distance, the ignored prophet reflects on why the Israelites wouldn't listen when he warned them that the Babylonian kings would conquer the city. He purses his lips bitterly, and his downturned mouth is accentuated by his plunging neck muscle and sagging shoulders. The folds in the clothes are very deep, evoking the anger, sorrow, and disgust that Jeremiah feels but cannot share, as it is too late.

Movement, realism, and human drama were Donatello's great contributions to sculpture.

Andrea Pisano (and others)—*Campanile Panels* (c. 1334-1359)

These 28 hexagonal and 28 diamond-shaped, blue-glazed panels decorated the Campanile, seven per side (where copies stand today). The original design scheme was perhaps Giotto's, but his successor, Andrea Pisano, and assistants executed most of the panels.

The panels celebrate technology, showing workers, inventors, and

Pisano's panels once adorned the Campanile.

Detail of a Pisano panel

Pop. 100,000...But Still a Small Town

At the dawn of the Renaissance, Florence was bursting with creative geniuses, all of who knew each other and worked together. For example, after Ghiberti won the bronze-door competition, Brunelleschi took teenage Donatello with him to Rome. Donatello returned to join Ghiberti's workshop. Ghiberti helped Brunelleschi with dome plans. Brunelleschi, Donatello, and Luca della Robbia collaborated on the Pazzi Chapel. And so on, and so on.

thinkers. Allegorically, they depict humanity's long march to "civilization"—a blend of art and science, brain and brawn. But realistically, they're snapshots of the industrious generation that helped Florence bounce back ferociously from the Black Death of 1348.

The lower **hexagonal panels** (reading clockwise) show God starting the chain of creation by inventing (1) man and (2) woman, then (3) Adam and Eve continuing the work, (4) Jabal learning to domesticate sheep, (5) Jubal blowing a horn, inventing music...

▶ *Continuing along the next wall...*

(6) Tubalcain the blacksmith and (7) Noah inventing wine and Miller Time. (8) An astronomer sights along a quadrant to chart the heavens and the (round, tilted-on-axis, pre-Columbian) earth, (9) a master builder supervises his little apprentices building a brick wall, (10) a doctor holds a flask of urine to the light for analysis (yes, that's what it is), and so on.

▶ *Skip ahead to the fourth wall, the second panel.*

(20) The invention of sculpture, as a man chisels a figure to life.

The upper **diamond-shaped panels,** made of marble on blue majolica (tin-glazed pottery tinged blue with copper sulfate), add religion (sacraments and virtues) to the civilization equation.

▶ *Another gallery is dedicated to the dome that defined the Florentine Renaissance (and the man who built it).*

Gallery of Brunelleschi's Dome

Model of the Lantern (Cupola di S. Maria del Fiore)
This model, done by Brunelleschi, shows only the dome's top portion.

Brunelleschi's actual dome, a feat of engineering that was both functional and beautiful, put mathematics in stone. It rises 330 feet from the ground, with eight white, pointed-arch ribs, filled in with red brick and capped with a "lantern" (cupola) to hold it all in place.

In designing the dome, Brunelleschi faced a number of challenges: The dome had to cover a gaping 140-foot hole in the roof of the church (a drag on rainy Sundays), a hole too wide to be spanned by the wooden scaffolding that traditionally supported a dome under construction. (An earlier architect suggested supporting the dome with a great mound of dirt inside the church...filled with coins, so peasants would later cart it away for free.) In addition, the eight-sided "drum" that the dome was to rest on was too weak to support its weight, and there were no side buildings on the church on which to attach Gothic-style buttresses.

The solution was a dome within a dome, leaving a hollow space between to make the structure lighter. And the dome had to be self-supporting, both while being built and when finished, so as not to require buttresses.

Brunelleschi used wooden models such as these to demonstrate his ideas to skeptical approval committees.

Scaffolding

Although no scaffolding supported the dome itself, the stonemasons needed exterior scaffolding to stand on as they worked. Support timbers were stuck into postholes in the drum (some are visible on the church today).

The dome rose in rings. First, the workers stacked a few blocks of white marble to create part of the ribs, then connected the ribs with horizontal crosspieces before filling in the space with red brick, in a herringbone pattern. When the ring was complete and self-supporting, they'd move the scaffolding up and do another section.

Tools

The dome weighs 80 million pounds—as much as the entire population of Florence—so Brunelleschi had to design special tools and machines to lift and work all that stone. (The lantern alone—which caps the dome—is a marble building nearly as tall as the Baptistery.) You'll see sun-dried bricks, brick molds, rope, a tool belt, compasses, stone pincers, and various

Model of the lantern that caps the Duomo

Brunelleschi, multitalented Renaissance Man

pulleys for lifting. Brunelleschi also designed a machine (not on display) that used horses to turn a shaft that reeled in rope, lifting heavy loads.

The dome was completed in 16 short years, capping 150 years of construction on the church. Brunelleschi enjoyed the dedication ceremonies, but he died before the lantern was completed. His legacy is a dome that stands as a proud symbol of man's ingenuity, proving that art and science can unite to make beauty.

Brunelleschi's Death Mask *(Maschera Funebre)*

Filippo Brunelleschi (1377-1446) was uniquely qualified to create the dome. Trained in sculpture, he gave it up in disgust after losing the gig for the Baptistery doors. In Rome, he visualized placing the Pantheon on top of Florence's Duomo, and dissected the Pantheon's mathematics and engineering.

Back home, he astounded Florence with a super-realistic painting of the Baptistery, as seen from the Duomo's front steps. Florentines lined up to see the painting (now lost) displayed side by side with the real thing, marveling at the 3-D realism. (Brunelleschi's mathematics of linear perspective were later expanded and popularized by the learned humanist Leon Battista Alberti.)

In 1420 Brunelleschi was declared *capomaestro* of the dome project. He was a jack-of-all-trades and now master of all as well, overseeing every aspect of the dome, the lantern, and the machinery to build them. Despite all his planning, it's clear from documentary evidence that he was making it up as he went along, exuding confidence to workers and city officials while privately improvising.

Rest of the Museum

Browse around the museum's three floors to find displays about other aspects of the remarkable church.

Silver Altar

The exquisite half-ton silver altarpiece honoring John the Baptist, which dominates this room, once stood in the Baptistery. Each of the immaculately restored silver panels depicts an episode from John the Baptist's life: birth, baptizing Jesus, and so on. Around the right side are his execution and the presentation of his disembodied head to Herod during a feast.

Altarpieces and Relics

These medieval **altarpieces,** which once adorned chapels and altars inside the Duomo, show saints and angels suspended in a gold never-never land. In the adjoining room, ornate reliquaries hold bones and objects of the saints (Peter's chains, Jerome's jawbone, and so on), many bought from a single, slick 14th-century con artist preying on medieval superstition.

In the 1400s, tastes changed, and these symbols of crude medievalism

Medieval altarpiece of *St. Sebastian*

were purged from the Duomo and stacked in storage. Soon artists replaced the golden heavenly scenes with flesh-and-blood humans who inhabited the physical world of rocks, trees, and sky...the Renaissance.

Among the **relics,** you may find a reliquary holding John the Baptist's finger. This severed index finger of the beheaded prophet is the most revered relic of all the holy body parts in this museum.

▸ *Various models, diagrams, paintings, and photos chart the multicentury...*

Evolution of the Facade

In 1587, the medieval facade by Arnolfo was considered hopelessly outdated and torn down like so much old linoleum. But work on a replacement never got off the ground, and the front of the church sat bare for nearly 300 years while church fathers debated proposal after proposal (like the models in this room) by many famous architects.

Finally, in the 1800s, as Italy was unifying and filled with a can-do spirit, there was a push to finish the facade. Emilio De Fabris (you may see his portrait) built a neo-Gothic facade (dedicated in 1887) that echoed the original work of Arnolfo. Critics may charge that De Fabris' facade is too retro, but it was the style of the church beloved by Ghiberti, Donatello, Brunelleschi, and the industrious citizens of Florence's Quattrocento, who saw it as Florence's finest art gallery.

The Opera del Duomo Today

If you climb all the way up to the sparse third-floor landing, you might see lab-coated workers busy in the restoration studio. They belong to the Opera del Duomo, the organization that does the continual work required to keep the cathedral's art in good repair (*opera* is Italian for "work").

For another behind-the-scenes peek, make one more stop after leaving the Duomo Museum: Head a half-block south to the **Opera del Duomo art studio** at Via dello Studio #23a (✪ see map on page 19). You can look through the open doorway and see workers sculpting new statues, restoring old ones, or making exact copies. They're carrying on an artistic tradition that dates back to the days of Brunelleschi. The "opera" continues.

Sights

Florence has more high-powered sights and museums per kilometer than any city in Europe. Though the city is small, I've clustered sights into "neighborhoods" (e.g., North of the Duomo) to make your sightseeing more efficient. Remember that some of Florence's biggest sights (marked with a ✪) are described in much more detail in the individual walks and tours chapters.

A few quick tips: Make reservations or buy a Firenze Card to avoid lines at the Uffizi and Accademia. Many sights are closed Monday and close early on Sunday. Some sights have erratic hours, so get the most up-to-date list at the Florence TI and read the fine print. Modest dress is required at some churches. ✪ See page 168 for more tips.

Despite the crowds, Florence prides itself on its gentility and grace under pressure. Be flexible.

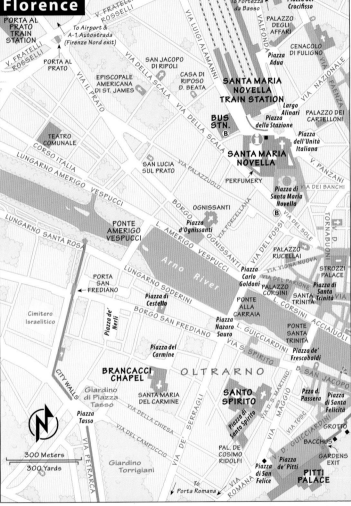

Florence

PORTA AL PRATO TRAIN STATION

V. FRATELLI ROSSELLI

V. FRATELLI ROSSELLI

PORTA AL PRATO

To Airport & A-1 Autostrada (Firenze Nord exit)

V. LUIGI ALAMANNI

VIA IL PRATO

EPISCOPALE AMERICANA DI ST. JAMES

VIA DELLA SCALA

SAN JACOPO DI RIPOLI

CASA DI RIPOSO D. BEATA

To Fortezza da Basso

Piazza del Crocifisso

PALAZZO DEGLI AFFARI

CENACOLO DI FULIGNO

Piazza Adua

VIA NAZIONALE

SANTA MARIA NOVELLA TRAIN STATION

VIA FAENZA

Largo Alinari

PALAZZO DEI CARTELLONI

Piazza della Stazione

BUS STN.

Piazza dell'Unità Italiana

SANTA MARIA NOVELLA

V. PANZANI

VIA DEI BANCHI

TEATRO COMUNALE

CORSO ITALIA

VIA DELLA SCALA

SAN LUCIA SUL PRATO

VIA PALAZZUOLO

PERFUMERY

Piazza di Santa Maria Novella

TORNABUONI

LUNGARNO AMERIGO VESPUCCI

BORGO OGNISSANTI

OGNISSANTI

Piazza d'Ognissanti

VIA PORCELLANA

VIA DEL SOLE

D.

LUNGARNO SANTA ROSA

PONTE AMERIGO VESPUCCI

L. AMERIGO VESPUCCI

Arno River

VIA DEL FOSSI

PALAZZO RUCELLAI

VIA VIGNA NUOVA

STROZZI PALACE

PORTA SAN FREDIANO

LUNGARNO SODERINI

Piazza di Cestello

BORGO SAN FREDIANO

Piazza de' Nerli

Piazza Carlo Goldoni

VIA DEL PARIONE

PALAZZO CORSINI

Piazza di Santa Trinita

PONTE ALLA CARRAIA

L. CORSINI

SANTA TRINITA

Cimitero Israelitico

Piazza Nazaro Sauro

L. GUICCIARDINI

PONTE SANTA TRINITA

PONTE ACCIAIUOLI

VIA S. SPIRITO

Piazza de' Frescobaldi

B. SAN JACOPO

CITY WALLS

Piazza del Carmine

OLTRARNO

BRANCACCI CHAPEL

Giardino di Piazza Tasso

SANTA MARIA DEL CARMINE

VIA DELLA CHIESA

VIA DE' SERRAGLI

SANTO SPIRITO

VIA S. MARTINO

VIA MAGGIO

Pza d. Passera

Piazza di Santa Felicita

Piazza di San Felice

VIA TOSO

GROTTO

BACCHUS

Piazza Tasso

VIA DEL CAMPUCCIO

Piazza di Santa Spirito

PAL. DE COSIMO RIDOLFI

VIA ROMANA

Piazza de' Pitti

PITTI PALACE

GARDENS EXIT

VIA PETRARCA

Giardino Torrigiani

To Porta Romana

D. GUICCIARDINI

N

300 Meters
300 Yards

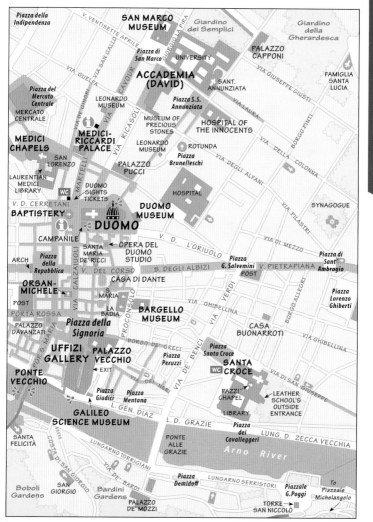

Piazza della Indipendenza

V. VENTISETTE APRILE

SAN MARCO MUSEUM

V. DORGOGNISSANTI

Giardino dei Semplici

Giardino della Gherardesca

VIA SAN GALLO

VIA GUELFA

VIA DE' GINORI

Piazza di San Marco

UNIVERSITY

PALAZZO CAPPONI

VIA GIUSEPPE GIUSTI

FAMIGLIA SANTA LUCIA

VIA CAVOUR

ACCADEMIA (DAVID)

SANT. ANNUNZIATA

Piazza del Mercato Centrale

LEONARDO MUSEUM

Piazza S.S. Annunziata

MERCATO CENTRALE

MEDICI CHAPELS

MUSEUM OF PRECIOUS STONES

HOSPITAL OF THE INNOCENTS

VIA LAURA

MEDICI-RICCARDI PALACE

VIA RICASOLI

LEONARDO MUSEUM

ROTUNDA

VIA DELLA COLONNA

SAN LORENZO

Piazza Brunelleschi

VIA DEGLI ALFANI

SYNAGOGUE

LAURENTIAN MEDICI LIBRARY

VIA MARTELLI

PALAZZO PUCCI

V. D. CERRETANI

DUOMO SIGHTS TICKETS

HOSPITAL

VIA FILASTRI

BAPTISTERY

WC

DUOMO MUSEUM

VIA DI MEZZO

DUOMO

CAMPANILE

SANTA MARIA DE' RICCI

OPERA DEL DUOMO STUDIO

V. D. L'ORIUOLO

Piazza G. Salvemini

V. PIETRAPIANA

Piazza di Sant' Ambrogio

ARCH

Piazza della Repubblica

VIA CALZAIUOLI

V. DEL CORSO

B. DEGLI ALBIZI

POST

ORSAN-MICHELE

CASA DI DANTE

VIA VERDI

Piazza Lorenzo Ghiberti

POST

S. MARIA LA BADIA

VIA GHIBELLINA

BORGO ALLEGRI

PORTA ROSSA

VIA PROCONSOLO

BARGELLO MUSEUM

CASA BUONARROTI

PALAZZO DAVANZATI

Piazza della Signoria

PALAZZO VECCHIO

VIA POR S. MARIA

BORGO DE' GRECI

Piazza Peruzzi

Piazza Santa Croce

VIA GHIBELLINA

UFFIZI GALLERY

EXIT

VIA DE' BENCI

SANTA CROCE

WC

VIA DI SAN GIUSEPPE

PONTE VECCHIO

VIA DEI NERI

Piazza Giudici

Piazza Mentana

PAZZI CHAPEL

LEATHER SCHOOL'S OUTSIDE ENTRANCE

GALILEO SCIENCE MUSEUM

L. GEN. DIAZ

LIBRARY

SANTA FELICITÀ

L. D. GRAZIE

Piazza dei Cavalleggeri

LUNG. D. ZECCA VECCHIA

PONTE ALLE GRAZIE

Arno River

Boboli Gardens

SAN GIORGIO

COSTA DI SAN GIORGIO

LUNGARNO TORRIGIANI

VIA DE' BARDI

Bardini Gardens

Piazza Demidoff

LUNGARNO SERRISTORI

Piazzale G. Poggi

To Piazzale Michelangelo

PALAZZO DE' MOZZI

TORRE SAN NICCOLÒ

The Duomo to the Arno River

Largely pedestrian-only and geared for tourists, this is Florence's sight-seeing core. To walk from the Duomo to the Arno takes 10 minutes, max. Many sights lie along the north-south spine of Via Calzaiuoli, easily connected by my ✪ Renaissance Walk.

▲▲Duomo (Cattedrale di Santa Maria del Fiore)

Florence's huge Gothic cathedral, or Duomo (from Latin *domus*— "house" of God), was built in medieval times and later topped with Filippo Brunelleschi's magnificent red-and-white dome that helped define the Renaissance.

The interior is huge and historic, but not worth a long wait to get in. The 500-foot-long, gray-and-white nave is the third longest in Christendom. Find busts of the Duomo's architects. Arnolfo di Cambio (left wall) started the church in 1296. Giotto (right wall) designed the Campanile (1330s). Brunelleschi (right wall) capped the church with the famous dome (c.1450). Finally, Emilio de Fabris (left wall) added the pink-green-white facade (1870s).

Above the main entrance is a huge clock, painted by Paolo Uccello (1443). It's a 24-hour clock, starting with sunset as the first hour, and turning counterclockwise.

Uccello's painting of John Hawkwood (left wall, colored green) wowed Florence with the 3-D illusion of an equestrian statue painted on a flat surface. A few steps up the nave is Florence's great poet Dante, with the city skyline in the distance.

At the altar, gaze up 300 feet into Brunelleschi's dome, which had to span a gaping 140-foot-wide hole. The vast dome is painted with the *Last Judgment* (by Vasari and Zuccari), where the dead rise into a multilevel heaven to be judged by a radiant Christ.

▶ *Free. Audioguide-€5. A combo-ticket (€15) covering the other Duomo sights can be purchased inside the cathedral, at the Duomo Museum, or at the main ticket office facing the Baptistery. Open Mon-Fri 10:00-17:00; Thu until 16:00 May and Oct, until 16:30 Nov-April; Sat 10:00-16:45, Sun 13:30-16:45. Facing the church, enter through the right-hand door in the Duomo's facade. English tours offered but fill up fast. Modest dress code enforced. Tel. 055-230-2885, www.operaduomo.firenze.it or www.museumflorence.com.*

Lines: Massive crowds line up to see the huge church, since it's a major sight (and free). Fortunately, the line moves fast.

✪ For more on the Duomo, see the Renaissance Walk.

▲Climbing the Duomo's Dome

Climb 463 steps to see: a grand view into the cathedral from the base of the dome; some of the traditional tools used in the dome's construction; Brunelleschi's innovative "dome-within-a-dome" construction; and finally, a glorious Florence-wide view from the top.

▶ *Covered by €15 combo-ticket and Firenze Card. Reservations required, available online at www.museumflorence.com or at ticket office opposite the Baptistery. Open Mon-Fri 8:30-19:00, Sat 8:30-17:40, closed Sun. Enter from outside the church on north side. Tel. 055-230-2885.*

✪ For more on the dome, see the Renaissance Walk.

▲Campanile (Giotto's Tower)

The 270-foot bell tower was designed by the great painter Giotto and decorated with statues by Donatello and others. Climb its 414 steps (somewhat easier and less crowded than climbing the Duomo's dome) for equally good views, including a view of that magnificent dome to boot.

▶ *€15 combo-ticket covers all Duomo sights; also covered by Firenze Card. Open daily 8:30-19:30, last entry 40 minutes before closing.*

✪ For more on the Campanile, see page 20 of the Renaissance Walk.

▲Baptistery

Nearly 1,000 years old, this building is most famous for its bronze doors. Lorenzo Ghiberti helped launch Renaissance perspective by depicting 3-D scenes on the doors' almost-flat surface. His north doors won a famous competition, while his east doors (facing the Duomo) were hailed by Michelangelo as the "Gates of Paradise."

Inside, sit and savor the medieval mosaic ceiling, where it's always Judgment Day, and Jesus is giving the ultimate thumbs-up and thumbs-down.

▶ *€15 combo-ticket covers all Duomo sights; also covered by Firenze Card. The interior is open Mon-Sat 11:15-19:00 except first Sat of month 8:30-14:00, Sun 8:30-14:00. The (fascimile) bronze doors are on the outside, so they are always viewable. Tel. 055-230-2885.*

✪ For more on the Baptistery, see the Renaissance Walk.

✪ For more on Ghiberti's famous doors, see the Duomo Museum Tour (with the original "Gates of Paradise").

▲▲▲Duomo Museum (Museo dell'Opera del Duomo)

Located behind the church (at Via del Proconsolo 9), the Duomo Museum is filled with some of the best sculpture of the Renaissance, including Michelangelo's *Pietà,* expressive Donatello statues, and Ghiberti's original bronze "Gates of Paradise" panels.

✪ See the Duomo Museum Tour.

▲▲▲Bargello (Museo Nazionale del Bargello)

This underappreciated sculpture museum has Donatello's prepubescent David, Michelangelo's *Bacchus,* and rooms of Medici treasures.

✪ See the Bargello Tour.

Casa di Dante (Dante's House)

Dante Alighieri (1265-1321), the poet who gave us *The Divine Comedy,* is the Shakespeare of Italy, the father of the modern Italian language, and the face on the country's €2 coin.

Dante lovers (but not everyone else) will appreciate this small, low-tech museum. It follows his life from his christening in Florence's Baptistery, to his spiritual awakening upon meeting his muse Beatrice, and the bitter years of political exile—never again to return to Florence. Homeless in Italy, Dante wrote his magnum opus, *The Divine Comedy,* which traces a pilgrim's journey through Hell and Purgatory, until—guided by a heavenly Beatrice—he's received into Paradise. For his landmark work, some call Dante the father of the Renaissance.

▸ *€4, covered by Firenze Card. Open April-Sept daily 10:00-18:00; Oct-March Tue-Sun 10:00-17:00, closed Mon. Near the Bargello at Via Santa Margherita 1. Tel. 055-219-416, www.museocasadidante.it.*

▲Orsanmichele Church

The exterior is a virtual sculpture gallery of Renaissance art (especially Donatello's *St. George*), and the peaceful interior has a glorious Gothic tabernacle.

✪ See page 26 of the Renaissance Walk.

▲Mercato Nuovo (a.k.a. the Straw Market)

This open-air loggia (c. 1550), originally a silk and straw market, is now a rustic yet touristy market. Its souvenirs are similar to those in the San Lorenzo market, but with firmer prices. Notice the circled X in the center, marking the spot where convicted criminals hit after being dropped from the ceiling. Find *Porcellino* (a statue of a wild boar), rub his nose, and "feed" him a coin, to ensure your return to Florence. Finish your visit at the food wagon in back, enjoying a traditional tripe sandwich. (Personally, I'd rather be dropped from the ceiling.)

▶ *Open daily. Located three blocks north of Ponte Vecchio on Via Calimala.*

▲Piazza della Repubblica

Lined with venerable cafes and high-fashion stores, this square has been a center of Florence for millennia. In Roman times, it was a fort at the intersection of the two main roads (marked today by the square's lone column). In 1571, Cosimo I de' Medici had the area walled in and made into the Jewish ghetto. If you venture outside the Piazza, you get a sense of what the old neighborhood was like—a tangle of narrow, winding lanes

Piazza della Repubblica, long a main intersection, is now a square surrounded by elegant cafés.

dotted with medieval towers. In the late 19th century, the area was razed to create this spacious square, with a huge triumphal arch celebrating the unification of Italy.

Today, people sip drinks at outdoor cafes, shop at the local La Rinascente department store, or enjoy a reasonably priced coffee on the store's rooftop terrace, with great Duomo and city views.

▲Palazzo Davanzati

This five-story, late-medieval tower house offers a rare look at a typical noble dwelling from the 14th century. The exterior is festooned with horse-tethering rings, torch holders, and poles for hanging laundry or flying flags. Inside, though the furnishings are pretty sparse, you'll see richly painted walls, fireplaces, a lace display, and even an indoor "outhouse."

▶ *€2, covered by Firenze Card. Open Tue-Sat 8:15-13:50, plus the first, third, and fifth Sun and second and fourth Mon of each month. Escorted visits (reservations required) show off still more rooms, usually at 10:00, 11:00, and 12:00. Located at Via Porta Rossa 13. Tel. 055-238-8610, www.polomuseale.firenze.it.*

▲▲▲Uffizi Gallery

The greatest collection of Italian paintings anywhere features masterworks by Giotto, Leonardo, Raphael, Titian, and Michelangelo, plus a roomful of Botticellis, including the *Birth of Venus.* Watch Western art evolve from stiff medieval altarpieces to three-dimensional Renaissance realism.

✪ See the Uffizi Gallery Tour.

▲▲Palazzo Vecchio

This castle-like fortress with the 300-foot spire dominates Florence's main square. In Renaissance times, it was the Town Hall, where citizens pioneered the once-radical notion of self-rule. Its official name—Palazzo della Signoria—refers to the elected members of the city council. In 1540, the tyrant Cosimo I de' Medici made the building his personal palace, redecorating the interior in lavish style. Today the building functions once again as the Town Hall, home to the mayor's office and the city council.

Entry to the ground-floor courtyard is free—step inside and feel the essence of the Medici.

Paying customers can see Cosimo's (fairly) lavish royal apartments, decorated with (fairly) top-notch paintings and statues by Michelangelo

Palazzo Vecchio, full of art and history   Galileo Science Museum has his finger.

(Victory) and Donatello *(Judith)*. The highlight is the Grand Hall, a 13,000-square-foot hall lined with huge frescoes of battle scenes by Giorgio Vasari. You can climb the tower (€10) for great views.

▶ *Museum—€10, covered by Firenze Card. Open April-Sept Fri-Wed 9:00-24:00, Thu 9:00-14:00; Oct-March Fri-Wed 9:00-19:00, Thu 9:00-14:00. Tel. 055-276-8224, http://museicivicifiorentini.comune.fi.it.*

✪ See page 29 of the Renaissance Walk.

▲Ponte Vecchio

Florence's oldest (1345), most famous, and most photogenic bridge has long been lined with shops—originally butcher shops, and now selling gold and silver.

✪ For more about the bridge, see page 35 of the Renaissance Walk.

▲▲Galileo Science Museum
(Museo Galilei e Istituto di Storia della Scienza)

Enough art, already! For a change of pace from statues and Madonnas, visit this collection of scientific curios, clocks, telescopes, maps, and turn-the-crank electrical contraptions, from A.D. 1000 to 1900. The museum is friendly, never crowded, and—ahhh!—wonderfully air-conditioned.

You'll see instruments of that trend-setting family, the Medici, who always seemed at the forefront of Europe's arts and sciences (Room I). Room II shows quadrants and astrolabes—navigation tools you'd point toward the horizon to triangulate your position relative to the stars. Room III has an 11-foot-tall armillary sphere, showing the earth surrounded by orbiting planets—the earth-centered view of the cosmos of medieval times.

The museum's highlight is the exhibit on Galileo Galilei (1564-1642), the groundbreaking scientist from Tuscany. Galileo was the first earthling to see the moons of Jupiter, using a homemade, 30-power telescope (the museum has several of his telescopes). You'll see his experiments on pendulum motion, falling objects, and an early thermoscope. Galileo was famously punished by the Church for claiming that the earth revolved around the sun. Appropriately, the museum's most talked-about exhibit is a jar containing Galileo's middle finger, raised eternally upward for all those blind to science.

▸ *€9, €22 family ticket, covered by Firenze Card. Open Wed-Mon 9:30-18:00, Tue 9:30-13:00. Located a block east of the Uffizi, at Piazza dei Giudici 1. Tel. 055-265-311, www.museogalileo.it.*

North of the Duomo

There are two sightseeing clusters—sights near the Accademia, and sights around the Basilica of San Lorenzo. Both are an easy 10-minute walk from the Duomo.

▲▲▲Accademia (Galleria dell'Accademia)

The star is Michelangelo's *David,* the consummate Renaissance statue of the buff, biblical shepherd boy taking on the giant. You'll also see the master's powerful (unfinished) *Prisoners.*

✪ See the Accademia Tour.

▲▲Museum of San Marco (Museo di San Marco)

This 15th-century monastery houses the greatest collection anywhere of the early Renaissance painter Fra Angelico (c.1395-1455). Fra Angelico (the "Angelic Brother") was the monastery's prior, known for his sweetness and humility (and beatified in 1984).

On the ground floor, the Hospice displays a dozen major altarpieces. His work fuses medieval styles (religious subjects, elaborate frames, serene faces, gold halos, and pious atmospheres) with Renaissance realism. Heavenly scenes are set in the Tuscan landscape, amid real-life flowers, trees, and distant hillsides. He uses bright primary colors (red-blue-yellow-gold) and meticulous, etched-in-glass detail. It's all evenly lit (with no moody shadows), creating a beautiful, mystical world—paintings that glow from within like stained glass windows.

Upstairs on the first floor are the monks' cells, or living quarters. Many

Fra Angelico work at Museum of San Marco   San Lorenzo church, home to Medici Chapels

were frescoed by Fra Angelico, particularly the 10 cells on your left as you venture down the corridor.

Don't miss the cells of Girolamo Savonarola (1452-1498), a later prior. This charismatic monk rode in from the Christian right, threw out the Medici, turned Florence into a theocracy, and sponsored "bonfires of the vanities" to burn books, paintings, and so on. You'll see his austere possessions—his simple wool clothes, blue Dominican cloak, rosary, crucifix, Bible, desk, and hair-shirt girdle. Finally, there's a stick snatched from the bonfire that burned Savonarola himself when Florence decided to change channels.

▶ *€4, free and crowded on first Sun of the month, covered by Firenze Card. Open Tue-Fri 8:15-13:50, Sat 8:15-16:50; also open 8:15-13:50 on first, third, and fifth Mon and 8:15-16:50 on second and fourth Sun of each month. Reservations possible but unnecessary. Located on Piazza San Marco, a block north of the Accademia. Tel. 055-238-8608, www.polomuseale.firenze.it.*

Museum of Precious Stones (Museo dell'Opificio delle Pietre Dure)

This unusual gem of a museum features exquisite mosaics of inlaid marble and other stones. The Medici loved colorful stone tabletops and floors, some featuring landscapes and portraits (find Cosimo I in Room I). Upstairs, you'll see wooden workbenches from the Medici workshop (1588), complete with foot-powered power tools. Rockhounds can browse 500 different stones (lapis lazuli, quartz, agate, marble, and so on) and the tools used to cut and inlay them.

▶ *€4, covered by Firenze Card. Open Mon-Sat 8:15-14:00, closed Sun.*

English descriptions. Located around the corner from the Accademia at Via degli Alfani 78, tel. 055-265-1357.

Basilica of San Lorenzo

The Basilica of San Lorenzo—on the site of the first Christian church in Florence—was built outside the Roman walls and consecrated in A.D. 393, then rebuilt in the early 1400s. The church anchors a complex of sights, described below: The Laurentian Medici Library (off a pleasant cloister) is along the left side and the Medici Chapels entrance is around back.

The church facade is big, ugly, and unfinished, because Pope Leo X (also a Medici) pulled the plug on Michelangelo's proposed makeover. Inside, the fresh spirit of 1420s Florence shines in Brunelleschi's perfectly symmetrical gray-and-white arches and diffused light. The Medici coat of arms (with the round pills of these "medics") decorates the ceiling, and everywhere are images of St. Lawrence, the Medici patron saint who was martyred on a grill.

Highlights of the church include two finely sculpted Donatello pulpits (in the nave) and Filippo Lippi's *Annunciation* (left transept). The Old Sacristy (far left corner)—designed by Brunelleschi, with bronze altar doors by Donatello—was a Medici burial chapel. Over the Sacristy's altar, a painted dome shows the exact arrangement of the heavens on July 4, 1442. Why that date? Scholars continue to speculate.

▸ *€4.50, €7 combo-ticket covers Laurentian Library, covered by Firenze Card. Buy tickets just inside cloister next door. Open Mon-Sat 10:00-17:30, Sun 13:30-17:30, covered by Firenze Card. The skippable San Lorenzo Museum (included in your church admission) features fancy reliquaries and Donatello's grave.*

Laurentian Medici Library

Designed by Michelangelo, it's best known for the impressive staircase, which widens imperceptibly as it descends. Michelangelo also did the surrounding walls, featuring empty niches, scrolls, and oddly tapering pilasters. Climb the stairs and enter the Reading Room—a long, rectangular hall with a coffered-wood ceiling—designed by Michelangelo to host scholars enjoying the Medici's collection of manuscripts.

▸ *€3, €7 combo-ticket with church, includes special exhibits. Generally open Mon-Sat 9:30-13:30, closed Sun.*

▲▲Medici Chapels (Cappelle Medicee)

The burial site of the Medici family stars Michelangelo's New Sacristy (1520-34). Michelangelo had spent his teen years living with the Medici, and here he paid them final tribute with monumental architecture, tombs, and brooding statues.

Your visit leads first into the big, domed (non-Michelangelo) Chapel of Princes (1602-1743), honoring later generations of Medici rulers.

Michelangelo's New Sacristy houses three Medici tombs. The Tomb of Lorenzo II (left wall, as you enter) depicts the grandson of Lorenzo the Magnificent as a Roman general atop a curved sarcophagus. Its two reclining statues are *Dusk* (a man, reflecting on the day's events) and *Dawn* (a woman, stirring restlessly after a long night). The Tomb of Giuliano (right wall) honors the son of Lorenzo the Magnificent. It features *Day* (a man, with every limb twisting in a different direction) and *Night* (a well-polished woman with coconut-shell breasts who does a crossover sit-up in her sleep). Together, the four statues represent the passage of Time.

The humble tomb on the entrance wall honors Lorenzo the Magnificent and his brother. Originally meant to be the grandest tomb, it was left unfinished, now topped with a Madonna and Child by Michelangelo. The Sacristy's altar wall has black doodles (behind glass), perhaps by Michelangelo. Michelangelo eventually abandoned the New Sacristy project to be pieced together by assistants.

As an architect, Michelangelo intended the room to symbolize how Time (the four reclining statues) kills mortal men (Lorenzo II and Giuliano), but through God's Grace (Madonna and Child), we can rise from the Earth (the ground

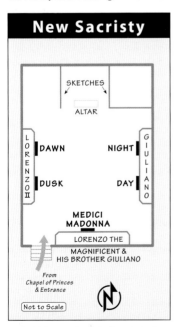

New Sacristy

SKETCHES

ALTAR

L O R E N Z O II

DAWN

NIGHT

G I U L I A N O

DUSK

DAY

MEDICI MADONNA

LORENZO THE MAGNIFICENT & HIS BROTHER GIULIANO

From Chapel of Princes & Entrance

Not to Scale

Day and *Night* recline in the Medici Chapels.

Medici-Riccardi Palace, the Medici home

floor) into the light (the dome overhead) of a glorious Heaven. Until then, Michelangelo's earth-bound statues squirm restlessly, pondering mortality but unable to come to terms with it.

▸ *€8 (or €6 if no special exhibits), free and crowded on first Sun of the month, covered by Firenze Card. Open Tue-Sat April-Oct 8:15-16:50, Nov-March 8:15-13:50; also open second and fourth Mon and first, third, and fifth Sun of each month. Reservations are possible but unnecessary (€3 fee). Audioguide-€6. Modest dress required. Enter at back side of Basilica of San Lorenzo. Tel. 055-238-8602, www.polomuseale. firenze.it.*

▲San Lorenzo Market

The vast open-air market sprawls down the streets ringing Mercato Centrale. Find lower-end leather, clothing, T-shirts, handbags, fake "Venetian" glass, silk ties, scarves, and Tuscan ceramics. Most of the leather stalls are run by Iranians selling South American leather that was tailored in Italy. Prices are soft, so go ahead and bargain.

▸ *Open daily 9:00-19:00, closed Mon in winter.*

▲Mercato Centrale (Central Market)

Florence's giant iron-and-glass-covered central market, a wonderland of picturesque produce, exudes a Florentine elegance. Enjoy generous free samples, watch pasta-making, graze fun eateries, and explore the sleek upscale food court upstairs. It's perfect for assembling a picnic, people-watching, and acquiring culinary souvenirs. Explore. You'll see parts of the cow (and bull) you'd never dream of eating (no, that's not a turkey neck).

▸ *Open Mon-Fri 7:00-14:00, Sat 7:00-17:00, closed Sun.*

Best Viewpoints

- The Campanile and the Duomo's dome (next to each other) and the tower at the Palazzo Vecchio offer the best views within the city.
- Piazzale Michelangelo (and San Miniato Church, above it) overlooks the city and the Duomo from the south side of the Arno River.
- Fiesole, a small town north of Florence, has panoramic hilltop views.
- La Rinascente department store, on Piazza Repubblica, has a reasonably priced top-floor terrace café.
- The Uffizi's café has cappuccino-friendly views of the Palazzo Vecchio and the Duomo.

▲Medici-Riccardi Palace (Palazzo Medici-Riccardi)

Built in 1444, this palace was home to the illustrious Medici family, including Lorenzo the Magnificent and Cosimo the Elder, as well as Michelangelo (who spent his teenage years here studying art). The palace also played host to many visitors, including Leonardo da Vinci (who played lute for Medici parties) and Botticelli (who studied the palace art). Soak up fading remnants of this historical ambience in the courtyard, the sculpture-studded garden, and Lorenzo's former workshop.

Upstairs is the highlight—the Chapel of the Magi. Benozzo Gozzoli's colorful frescoes of the *Procession of the Magi* (1459) are a snapshot of Renaissance Florence. The three Magi are dressed in the latest 15th-century fashions, and parade on horseback through a green, spacious Tuscan countryside. Find famous Medici in the frescoes. On the biggest wall is Cosimo the Elder (in a red hat, riding behind the curly-haired king). Behind Cosimo, find 10-year-old Lorenzo the Magnificent (sixth in from the left, with red cap, scoop nose, bowl-cut hair, and intense gaze). Above Lorenzo (and slightly to the left) is Gozzoli himself.

The palace also has a few partially furnished rooms, a Madonna and Child by Fra Filippo Lippi, and a Baroque ceiling fresco by Luca Giordano. Today, the palace functions as a county government building, so you may encounter bureaucrats at work.

▶ *€7, cash only, covered by Firenze Card. Open Thu-Tue 8:30-19:00, closed Wed. The ticket entrance is north of the main gated courtyard.*

Videoguide-€4. Located at Via Cavour 3, a long block north of the Duomo. Tel. 055-276-0340, www.palazzo-medici.it.

Leonardo Museums

Two different-but-similar entrepreneurial establishments several blocks apart show off replicas of Leonardo's ingenious inventions and experiments. While there are no actual historic artifacts, you can see a full-size armored tank, walk into a chamber of mirrors, operate a rotating crane, or watch experiments in flying. There are English descriptions, and you're encouraged to play with the models—great for kids. Either museum is fun for anyone who wants to crank the shaft of Leonardo's fertile imagination.

▶ *Museo Leonardo da Vinci (€7, €0.50 discount with this book) is open daily 10:00-19:00, Nov-March until 18:00. Located at Via dei Servi 66 red. Tel. 055-282-966, www.mostredileonardo.com.*

  Le Macchine di Leonardo da Vinci (€7, €2 discount with this book) is open daily 9:30-19:30. Located in Galleria Michelangelo at Via Cavour 21. Tel. 055-295-264, www.macchinedileonardo.com.

East of the Duomo

The landmark of this less-visited area is Santa Croce church, a gathering spot in this (slightly rundown) neighborhood.

▲▲Santa Croce Church

One of Florence's biggest and oldest churches (begun in 1294), Santa Croce houses groundbreaking art and the tombs of great Florentines.

  The spacious 375-foot nave is lined with tall columns and wide, airy arches. On the left side is the tomb of Galileo, the scientist who served Florence's Grand Duke. On the right side are Michelangelo (who grew up a block west of here and attended Santa Croce), Dante (a memorial to the hometown poet), Machiavelli (who penned a how-to manual of hardball politics), and Rossini (who composed the *William Tell Overture*).

  To the right of the main altar is Giotto's *Death of St. Francis* (c. 1325). With simple but eloquent gestures, Francis' brothers kneel to bid the charismatic monk a sad farewell. It's one of the first expressions of human emotion in modern painting, foreshadowing the Renaissance.

  You'll find St. Francis' brown robe preserved in a gold frame in the sacristy (just outside the right transept) and Cimabue's expressive (if flood-damaged) *Crucifixion* (1423). Nearby, evocative photos show the

Santa Croce—tombs, frescoes, architecture

S. M. Novella—Masaccio's 3-D fresco

horrendous damage of the Arno floods (1966). A hallway leads to a leather school, where poor people make leather goods for sale.

Exit into the cloister, with the domed Pazzi Chapel (1430). Brunelleschi's circle-in-square design, simple white-and-gray color scheme, and perfect geometry capture the Renaissance in miniature. The Museum (included with admission) has Gaddi's 1,300-square-foot *Tree of the Cross and Last Supper*. Medieval monks could sit beneath this Last Supper and imagine they were eating in the company of Jesus.

▶ *€6 (€8.50 combo-ticket with Casa Buonarroti), covered by Firenze Card. Open Mon-Sat 9:30-17:30, Sun 14:00-17:30, multimedia guide-€6. Modest dress required. Located a 10-minute walk east of the Palazzo Vecchio along Borgo de' Greci. Tel. 055-246-6105, www.santacroce opera.it.*

Avoid lines by buying your ticket from the leather school at the back end of the church. To get there, enter the passageway at Via San Giuseppe 5 red, and follow signs through the parking lot to the low-key back entrance. Don't be shy—they want you to visit their store. Once inside, pass through the workshops to the sales room with the cash register, buy a church ticket, and head down the hallway that leads into the church.

Casa Buonarroti (Michelangelo's House)

This museum, standing on property once owned by Michelangelo, displays some of Michelangelo's early, less-than-monumental statues and a few sketches.

Climb the stairs, where you come face-to-face with portraits (by his contemporaries) of 60-year-old Michelangelo. Also displayed are some walking sticks and leather shoes thought to be Michelangelo's.

The museum's highlight is two relief panels, Michelangelo's earliest known sculptures. Teenage Michelangelo carved the *Battle of the Centaurs* (1490-1492), a squirming tangle of battling nudes, showing his fascination with anatomy. He kept this in his personal collection all his life. *The Madonna of the Stairs* (c. 1490) is as contemplative as *Centaurs* is dramatic. Throughout his long career, bipolar Michelangelo veered between these two styles—moving or still, emotional or thoughtful, pagan or Christian.

Nearby are the big wooden model (maybe by Michelangelo) of the never-completed facade of the Basilica of San Lorenzo and a model of a never-completed river god for the Medici Chapels. The museum also displays small clay and wax models—some by Michelangelo, some by pupils—used to sketch out ideas for statues. Finally, a darkened room shows off some of Michelangelo's sketches (a rotating display of their vast collection). Vasari claimed that Michelangelo wanted to burn his preliminary sketches, lest anyone think him less than perfect.

▶ *€6.50 (€8.50 combo-ticket with Santa Croce Church), covered by Firenze Card. Open Wed-Mon 10:00-17:00, closed Tue. English descriptions. Located at Via Ghibellina 70. Tel. 055-241-752, www.casa buonarroti.it.*

West of the Duomo

The train station and Church of Santa Maria Novella anchor this neighborhood a 10- to 15-minute walk from the Duomo.

▲▲Church of Santa Maria Novella

It's chock-full of art from medieval to Mannerist, including Masaccio's 3-D breakthrough, *The Trinity*.

The green-and-white facade is by Alberti, c. 1460. Inside, look down the nave for an optical illusion—the columns converge and get shorter as they approach the altar, making the 330-foot nave look even longer.

In the nave hangs Giotto's *Crucifixion* (c. 1300), a study in understated tragedy. View Masaccio's *Trinity* (c. 1427, on the left wall) from about 20 feet away, standing on the shield with a crown. From this perspective, it appears that Masaccio has blown a nine-foot-high hole in the church wall, creating a chapel visited by God, Jesus on the cross, and several mourners. The chapel's checkerboard ceiling converges at the back to create the

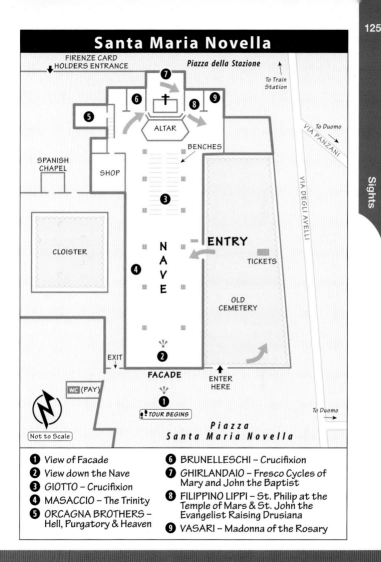

Santa Maria Novella

FIRENZE CARD HOLDERS ENTRANCE

Piazza della Stazione

To Train Station

VIA PANZANI — To Duomo

VIA DEGLI AVELLI

ALTAR

BENCHES

SPANISH CHAPEL

SHOP

CLOISTER

N A V E

ENTRY

TICKETS

OLD CEMETERY

EXIT

FACADE

ENTER HERE

WC (PAY)

Not to Scale

! TOUR BEGINS

Piazza Santa Maria Novella

To Duomo →

Sights

1. View of Facade
2. View down the Nave
3. GIOTTO – Crucifixion
4. MASACCIO – The Trinity
5. ORCAGNA BROTHERS – Hell, Purgatory & Heaven
6. BRUNELLESCHI – Crucifixion
7. GHIRLANDAIO – Fresco Cycles of Mary and John the Baptist
8. FILIPPINO LIPPI – St. Philip at the Temple of Mars & St. John the Evangelist Raising Drusiana
9. VASARI – Madonna of the Rosary

illusion of 3-D. Masaccio was the first painter since ancient times to portray real humans inhabiting a spacious, three-dimensional world.

In the left transept, a fresco of *Hell* (by the Orcagna brothers, c. 1350) shows naked souls begging for mercy—a grim scene right out of the bubonic plague that killed half of Florence. Brunelleschi's realistic wooden crucifix hangs in a chapel to the left of the altar.

Behind the altar are frescoes by Ghirlandaio. Though ostensibly about John the Baptist, they're a virtual snapshot of everyday life in Florence, circa 1490. Florentines in their Sunday best parade through three-dimensional video-game landscapes of Renaissance architecture.

Finally, in Filippino Lippi's *St. Philip* (in the chapel to the right of the altar), the Christian saint battles the pagan god Mars by unleashing...a farting dragon. Believe it when you see it.

▶ *€5, covered by Firenze Card. Open Mon-Thu 9:00-17:30, Fri 11:00-17:30, Sat 9:00-17:00, Sun 12:00-17:00 July-Sept (from 13:00 Oct-June), last entry 45 minutes before closing. Audioguide-€5. Modest dress required. Tel. 055-219-257, www.chiesasantamarianovella.it.*

Farmacia di Santa Maria Novella

Thick with the lingering aroma of centuries of spritzes, this palatial perfumery started as the herb garden of Santa Maria Novella and was founded by the Dominicans in 1612. Today it's a retail shop selling perfumes and herbal products. Well-known by locals for quality, it's extremely Florentine. Pick up the history sheet at the desk and wander deep into the shop. The third room dates from 1612 and offers a peek at one of Santa Maria Novella's cloisters. Gaze on its dreamy frescoes and imagine a time before Vespas and tourists.

▶ *Free, though shopping is encouraged. Open daily 9:00-20:00. Located a block west of Piazza Santa Maria Novella, 100 yards down Via della Scala at #16. Tel. 055-216-276, www.smnovella.com.*

South of the Arno River (Oltrarno)

The Arno River separates the city center from the Oltrarno—the neighborhood on the "other" *(altro)* side of the river. The two sides have historically been connected by the oldest bridge, Ponte Vecchio, lined with its characteristic shops.

Florence was born on the north bank (founded by the Romans in the first century B.C.). The Oltrarno grew in medieval times until, by

Michelangelo's day, it was as extensive as the north side. It's always been Florence's poorer, working-class cousin. It's grittier, more local, with more artisan shops and fewer tourists. During midafternoon siesta, many streets look like a ghost town.

But it's an interesting look at a more authentic Florence, and it hosts several high-power sights—the Pitti Palace, Santo Spirito Church, and Brancacci Chapel. To link these sights and see a few back lanes and local color, take the Oltrano Walk, described next.

▲Oltrarno Walk

The map on page 128 traces the following route. The walk takes 90 minutes (plus any sightseeing inside the Pitti Palace, Brancacci Chapel, and Santo Spirito Church). It's best mornings or evenings—midafternoon is hot, and many churches and shops are closed.

From the Ponte Vecchio, *head west on Borgo San Jocopo.* Pause at the twin medieval towers, typical of the countless family towers that dotted 12th-century Florence's skyline. Hotel Lungarno's riverside viewpoint offers a great photo-op of the Ponte Vecchio.

Turn left on tiny Via Toscanella, a quiet laundry-draped lane. You'll pass artisan shops plying generations-old trades—making handmade furniture, leather goods, pottery, picture frames, bookbinding. If the door's open, step in and politely ask, *Posso guardare?*—"Can I take a look?"

At the end of Via Toscanella, to the left is the Pitti Palace. *Turn right on Sdrucciolo de' Pitti* to reach Piazza Santo Spirito—with its church and trendy-but-seedy ambience.

Head northwest on Via S. Agostino, walking 5-10 minutes to the Brancacci Chapel. The neighborhoods around the church are considered the last surviving bits of old Florence.

Head north a long block and turn right on Borgo San Frediano, which becomes Via Santo Spirito. Pause at Piazza de' Frescobaldi to admire a picturesque Medici-era fountain, and to marvel at how the traffic chaos all seems to work out fine. Continuing on, the rough-around-the-edges neighborhood becomes more upscale and pedestrian-friendly. Look! There are the twin towers again, the street becomes Borgo San Jacopo, and—just like that—you're back at Ponte Vecchio. *Ciao.*

▲▲Pitti Palace

The imposing Pitti Palace has many separate museums and two huge

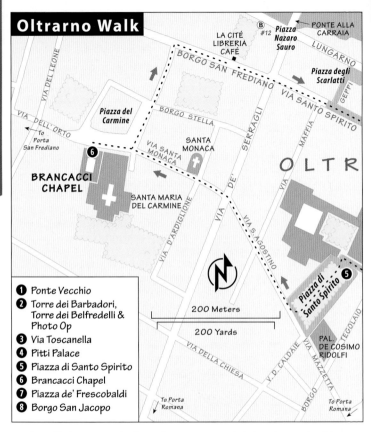

Oltrarno Walk

1 Ponte Vecchio
2 Torre dei Barbadori,
   Torre dei Belfredelli &
   Photo Op
3 Via Toscanella
4 Pitti Palace
5 Piazza di Santo Spirito
6 Brancacci Chapel
7 Piazza de' Frescobaldi
8 Borgo San Jacopo

gardens. Trying to see it all can be more overwhelming than enjoyable. Focus on the Palatine Gallery—Florence's second-best collection of paintings—starring Raphael Madonnas and Titian portraits.

The plain and brutal facade is more than two football fields long. Enter and climb the stairs to reach the…

Palatine Gallery: To see the highlights, walk straight down the spine (avoiding side rooms), then make a U-turn and double back through a

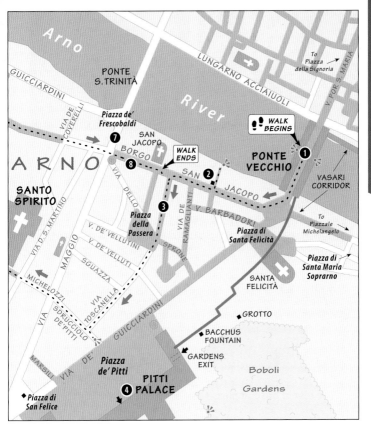

dozen more. In Room 1, a bust of Cosimo I de' Medici honors the ruler who made the palace (arguably) the center of European culture for a century (c. 1550-1650). Gaze out the windows at the expansive, statue-studded Boboli Gardens, the model for Versailles.

Stroll through palatial rooms with frescoed ceilings and floor-to-ceiling paintings in gilded frames. In Room 17 you'll run into a fireplace topped

Lippi's round *Madonna* at the Pitti

Brancacci Chapel, Masaccio's masterwork

with Lippi's *Madonna and Child* (c.1452), considered the first round-framed Renaissance painting.

Continue to the far end, double back, and enter Rooms 27-28, highlighting Raphael (Raffaelo). His Madonna-and-Childs are dreamy, bathed in even light, with smooth brushwork and restrained colors. By contrast, his portraits are photo-realistic, showing plain faces and human imperfections. Still, everything is geometrically perfect: Women have oval faces, sitters are posed at the best three-quarter angle, and Holy Families stand in pyramid-shaped groups.

Rooms 31-32 focus on the portraits of Titian (Tiziano). With rich colors, exuberant motion, and (in later works) rough brushwork, Titian captured Renaissance sophisticates in all their sensual glory. Find his passionate *Mary Magdalene,* the *Portrait of a Man* with piercing blue eyes, and the richly dressed *Portrait of a Lady.*

Included in admission are the Royal Apartments. Ogle rooms of velvety wallpaper, chandeliers, and canopied beds, each a different style and color. Here is the splendor of the Florentine dukes that inspired Europe.

The rest of the complex: It'd be a Pitti to miss the Boboli Gardens. See its statue-ringed amphitheater, the melted-frosting Grotto, and the much-photographed fountain of an obese Bacchus.

▶ *To see the Palatine Gallery, buy ticket #1—€13 (€8.50 if no special exhibitions), covered by Firenze card. The Palatine is open Tue-Sun 8:15-18:50, closed Mon. The gardens and other museums have similar (but not identical) hours and prices. Tel. 055-238-8614, www.polomuseale.firenze.it.*

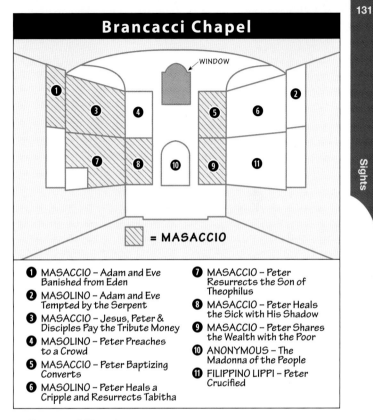

Brancacci Chapel

= MASACCIO

1. **MASACCIO** – Adam and Eve Banished from Eden
2. **MASOLINO** – Adam and Eve Tempted by the Serpent
3. **MASACCIO** – Jesus, Peter & Disciples Pay the Tribute Money
4. **MASOLINO** – Peter Preaches to a Crowd
5. **MASACCIO** – Peter Baptizing Converts
6. **MASOLINO** – Peter Heals a Cripple and Resurrects Tabitha
7. **MASACCIO** – Peter Resurrects the Son of Theophilus
8. **MASACCIO** – Peter Heals the Sick with His Shadow
9. **MASACCIO** – Peter Shares the Wealth with the Poor
10. **ANONYMOUS** – The Madonna of the People
11. **FILIPPINO LIPPI** – Peter Crucified

▲▲Brancacci Chapel

In 1424, 23-year-old Masaccio began frescoing the Brancacci Chapel, where he virtually invented the 3-D realism that defines Western art.

Of the dozen-or-so scenes (mostly about St. Peter), roughly half are by Masaccio and half by his less-talented colleague, Masolino.

In Masaccio's *Adam and Eve* (left wall, upper left), Adam buries his face in shame while Eve wails from deep within. These simple human gestures speak louder than any medieval symbolism.

In *The Tribute Money* (left wall, upper level), Jesus and his disciples inhabit a spacious world, defined by mountains, the lake, trees, and buildings. They cast late-afternoon shadows to the left, seemingly lit by the same light we are—the natural light from the Brancacci's window. By fixing where we the viewers are in relation to these figures, Masaccio lets us stand in the presence of the human Jesus.

In *Peter Heals the Sick* (center wall, left of window), the saint walks toward us along a Florentine street. Masaccio's people are not generic saints but distinct individuals (like the old bald guy). They exude seriousness, deep in thought, as though hit with a spiritual two-by-four. Masaccio's ordinary-but-dignified people helped Renaissance-era Florentines shape their own self-image.

Masolino's work, by contrast, reflects an earlier style. The colorful *Peter Heals a Cripple* (right wall, upper level) shows two well-dressed dandies sashaying across a square. Their cardboard-cutout weightlessness, evenly lit cheeriness, and intricately patterned clothes are textbook International Gothic.

Back to Masaccio. Find his self-portrait in *Peter Resurrects the Son of Theophilus* (left wall, lower level). At the far right, Masaccio painted fellow artists Brunelleschi (farthest right, with black headdress), Alberti (slightly to the left), and himself (looking out at us). By the time Masaccio died at 27—the same age as Hendrix, Morrison, Cobain, and Winehouse—he'd rocked the world of art.

▶ *€6 (cash only), covered by Firenze Card. Although reservations are required, on weekdays and any day off-season it's often possible to walk right in, especially if you come before 15:30. Open Mon and Wed-Sat 10:00-17:00, Sun 13:00-17:00, closed Tue, last entry 45 minutes before closing. Videoguide-€2. Free 20-minute film has English subtitles. Located in the Church of Santa Maria del Carmine. Reservations tel. 055-276-8224 or 055-276-8558, ticket desk tel. 055-284-361, http://museicivicifiorentini.comune.fi.it.*

Santo Spirito Church

Within this church is an interior by Brunelleschi—pure Renaissance. (Ignore the ornate Baroque altar, added later.) Notice Brunelleschi's "dice"—the stone cubes above the column capitals that contribute to the nave's playful lightness.

The church's art treasure is a painted, carved wooden crucifix

(Crocifisso) attributed to 17-year-old Michelangelo. The sculptor donated this early work to the monastery in appreciation for allowing him to dissect and learn about bodies. It's in the sacristy, through a door midway down the left side of the nave (if it's closed, ask someone to let you in). Copies of Michelangelo's *Pietà* and *Risen Christ* flank the nave (near the main door). Beer-drinking, guitar-playing rowdies decorate the church steps.

▶ *Free. Open Thu-Tue 9:30-12:30 & 16:00-17:30, except Sun when it opens at 11:30, closed Wed. Tel. 055-210-030.*

▲Piazzale Michelangelo

Overlooking the city from the south side of the river, this square with a huge statue of *David* has a stunning view of Florence. An inviting café is just below the overlook. The best photo-op is from the street immediately below the overlook. Off the west side of the piazza is a quiet terrace. After dark, the square is packed with teenagers licking ice cream and each other.

About 200 yards uphill is the stark, beautiful, crowd-free, Romanesque San Miniato Church. Highlights include the "carpet of marble" floor, a colorful Renaissance tabernacle, the exquisitely painted Chapel of Cardinal Jacopo (left side of the nave), and the tomb of St. Minias (downstairs in the crypt). Upstairs, the sacristy has frescoes (c. 1350) showing St. Benedict—his arm always outstretched—busy blessing, preaching, chasing the devil, and founding his order of monks.

▶ *The piazza is a 30-minute uphill hike from Ponte Vecchio. Or take bus #12 from the train station (30 minutes) or a taxi from Ponte Vecchio. Then enjoy the easy, pleasant downhill walk back into town: From the piazza (uphill side), take the steps between the two bars and head down Via San Salvatore al Monte.*

▲Fiesole

Three miles north of downtown Florence, this tiny town perched on a hill overlooking the Arno valley offers great views and a pleasant respite. There's little more to Fiesole (fee-AY-zoh-lay) than a main square (where the bus stops), a few restaurants and shops, a few minor sights...and that great view.

For the best panorama, hike uphill from the main square on Via San Francesco (10 minutes) to the view terrace near La Reggia restaurant. A little farther up is the Church of San Francesco, with colorful altar paintings.

▶ *Getting There: From Florence's Piazza San Marco, take bus #7—past vineyards and villas—to the last stop, Piazza Mino (30-minute ride, 3-4/hour, fewer after 21:00, €1.20—€2 if bought on bus). A taxi costs €25-35. The TI is near the main square, behind the Fiesole Duomo at Via Portigiani 3, tel. 055-596-1311, www.fiesoleforyou.it.*

Side Trips from Florence

The following destinations are doable as side-trips from Florence. But they'll be much more satisfying with an overnight or as part of a longer Italian itinerary.

Tuscan Hill Towns

Tuscany is speckled with sun- and wine-soaked villages clinging to hill-tops, amid rolling farmlands. Of the many sightseeing options, here are a handful of places within 90 minutes of Florence by bus or train. To see more, rent a car.

▲▲▲**Siena:** This red-brick hilltop city is known for its pageantry, Palio horse race, art-filled Duomo, traffic-free ambience, and stunning main square—great anytime but best after dark. Siena is 75 minutes from Florence by *"rapida/via superstrada"* bus (2/hour), which is faster than the train. For those staying the night in Siena, a hotel-to-hotel taxi ride can be a good value for small groups with luggage (around €120).

▲**Pisa:** Snap a photo of yourself propping up the iconic Leaning Tower, breeze through the nearby Duomo and Baptistery on the grassy Field of Miracles...and move on. Pisa is an easy hour away on the train.

▲**Lucca:** Charming city with a lively (and flat) town center, ringed by intact old walls wide enough for biking and strolling. It's 90 minutes by train.

Cortona: This classic (and touristy) hill town under the Tuscan sun, with its historic churches, Etruscan sights, and Medici Fortress, is easily reached by 90-minute direct train from Florence.

▲▲▲Rome

A 90-minute express train (may require seat reservation) can whisk you into the heart of the Eternal City.

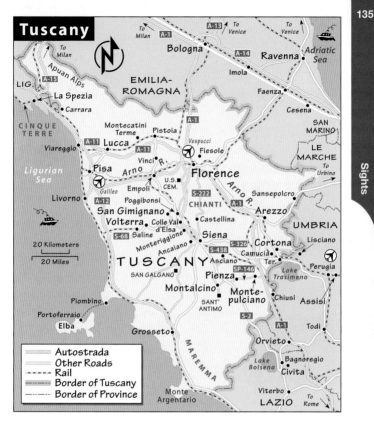

Tuscany

To Milan

A-13 To Venice

To Venice

A-1

To Milan

Bologna

A-14

Ravenna

Adriatic Sea

Apuan Alps

EMILIA-ROMAGNA

Imola

LIG.

A-15

La Spezia

Carrara

Faenza

Cesena

CINQUE TERRE

Montecatini Terme

Pistoia

SAN MARINO

A-1

Lucca

A-11

Vespucci

LE MARCHE

Viareggio

A-11

Fiesole

Pisa

Arno R.

Florence

To Urbino

Ligurian Sea

Galileo

Empoli

U.S. CEM.

Arno R.

Sansepolcro

Livorno

Poggibonsi

S-222

CHIANTI

A-1

Arezzo

A-12

San Gimignano

Volterra

Colle Val d'Elsa

Castellina

UMBRIA

20 Kilometers

Saline

Monteriggione

Siena

S-326

Cortona

Lisciano

20 Miles

Ancaiano

TUSCANY

Asciano

S-438

Camucia

Ter.

Perugia

SAN GALGANO

SP-146

Pienza

Lake Trasimeno

Piombino

Montalcino

SANT' ANTIMO

Monte-pulciano

Chiusi

Assisi

Portoferraio

Elba

S-2

A-1

Todi

Grosseto

Orvieto

MAREMMA

Lake Bolsena

Bagnoregio

Civita

Monte Argentario

Viterbo

To Rome

LAZIO

Autostrada

Other Roads

Rail

Border of Tuscany

Border of Province

Sleeping

Florence is so compact that all of my recommended hotels are within walking distance of major sights. From Florence's train station, most are a 10- to 15-minute walk or €6-8 taxi ride away. I like hotels that are clean, central, a good value, and friendly, with local character and simple facilities that don't cater to American "needs."

Double rooms listed in this book average around €140, ranging from €50 (very simple, toilet and shower down the hall) to €450 (maximum plumbing and more). Many Florentine hotels offer a combination of Old World ambience—wood-beam ceilings, frescoes, and antique furniture—with all the modern conveniences.

Hotel Price Code

$$$ Most rooms are €160 or more.
$$ Most rooms €100–160.
$ Most rooms €100 or less.

These rates are for a standard double room with bath during high season. Unless otherwise noted, breakfast is included, the hotels have an elevator and air-conditioning, and Wi-Fi is generally free.

A Typical Florence Hotel Room

A €140 double room in Florence is small by American standards and has one double bed or two twins. There's probably a bathroom in the room with a toilet, sink, and bathtub or shower. Rooms generally have a telephone and TV, and may have a safe. Most hotels at this price will have air-conditioning—cheaper places may not. Breakfast is generally included. It's usually a self-service buffet of cereal, ham, cheese, yogurt, and juice, while a server takes your coffee order.

The hotel will likely have Internet access, either Wi-Fi or a guest computer in the lobby. The staff speaks at least enough English to get by. Night clerks aren't paid enough to care deeply about problems that arise.

Making Reservations

Reserve as far in advance as you can, particularly if you'll be traveling during peak season (summer) or any major holidays. Make reservations by phone, through the hotel's website, or with an email that reads something like this:

Dear Hotel Florence,

I would like to reserve a double room for 2 people for 3 nights, arriving 19 July and departing 22 July. If possible, I would like a quiet room with a double bed (not twin beds), a Duomo view, and a shower (not a tub). Please let me know if you have a room available and the price. Thank you.

Some hoteliers can reserve entry times for the Uffizi and Accademia—ask when you book.

If the hotel requires your credit-card number for a deposit, you can send it by email (I do), but it's safer via phone, the hotel's secure website, or split between two emails. Once your room is booked, print out the confirmation, and reconfirm your reservation with a phone call or email a day or two in advance. If you must cancel your reservation, some hotels require advance notice or you'll be billed. Even if there's no penalty, it's polite to give at least three days' notice.

Budget Tips

Some of my listed hotels offer special rates to my readers—it's worth asking when you book your room.

To get the best rates, book directly with the hotel, not through a hotel-booking engine. Start with the hotel's website, looking for promo deals. Check rates every few days, as prices can vary greatly based on demand. Email several hotels to ask for their best price and compare offers—you may be astonished at the range. You may get a better rate if you offer to pay cash, stay at least three nights, skip breakfast, or simply ask if there are any cheaper rooms.

In addition to hotels, I also list a few alternatives. Bed-and-breakfasts (B&Bs) offer a private room in someone's home, often without a 24-hour reception, breakfast room, or public lounge. At nun-run convents, the beds are twins and English is often in short supply, but the price is right. Hostels offer €20-30 dorm beds and a few inexpensive doubles. Airbnb.com makes it reasonably easy to find a place to sleep in someone's home.

Don't be too cheap when picking a hotel. Cheaper places can be depressing, and Florence's intensity is easier to handle with a welcoming oasis to call home. Light sleepers should ask for a *tranquillo* room in the back. In summer, pay a little more for air-conditioning—to avoid both the heat and the mosquitos. If there's no air-conditioning, request a fan and a small plug-in bulb (zanzariere) to keep the bloodsuckers at bay.

THE DUOMO TO THE ARNO RIVER—Central as can be, amid sights and restaurants in the traffic-free core; slightly overpriced but worth it	
$$$ Palazzo Niccolini al Duomo Via dei Servi 2 | tel. 055-282-412 www.niccolinidomepalace.com	Elite historic residence with palatial lounge (free evening tea) and splendid rooms varying wildly in size
$$$ Hotel Duomo Piazza del Duomo 1 | tel. 055-219-922 www.hotelduomofirenze.it	Modern and comfortable enough; views of Duomo looming like a monster just outside
$$$ In Piazza della Signoria B&B Via dei Magazzini 2 | tel. 055-239-9546 www.inpiazzadellasignoria.com	Overlooking Palazzo Vecchio; peaceful, refined, homey; "partial view" not worth extra euros
$$$ Hotel Pendini Via degli Strozzi 2 | tel. 055-211-170 www.hotelpendini.it	Grand, classy-feeling Old World building overlooking Piazza della Repubblica
$$$ Hotel Davanzati Via Porta Rossa 5 | tel. 055-286-666 www.hoteldavanzati.it	Modern comforts plus artistic touches, cheerfully family-run, evening happy hour, loaner laptops
$$$ Hotel Torre Guelfa Borgo S.S. Apostoli 8 tel. 055-239-6338 www.hoteltorreguelfa.com	Regal public spaces, medieval tower with view, pricey but worth it (esp. Room 315)
$$$ Relais Uffizi Chiasso de Baroncelli/Chiasso del Buco 16 | tel. 055-267-6239 www.relaisuffizi.it	Peaceful little gem on alleyway, lounge overlooks magnificent Piazza della Signoria
$$ Soggiorno Battistero Piazza San Giovanni 1 | tel. 055-295-143 www.soggiornobattistero.it	7 simple, airy rooms; friendly owners, views over Baptistery or quieter in back
$$ Residenza Giotto B&B Via Roma 6 | tel. 055-214-593 www.residenzagiotto.it	6 bright, slightly scruffy, top-floor rooms on Florence's upscale shopping drag; great view terrace
$$ La Residenza del Proconsolo B&B Via del Proconsolo 18 black tel. 055-264-5657 www.proconsolo.com	5 older-feeling rooms, some Duomo views, nice large rooms, breakfast in room, no elevator

$$ Hotel Maxim Via de' Calzaiuoli 11 | tel. 055-217-474 www.hotelmaximfirenze.it	Reasonably priced, straightforward rooms in prime location; painting-lined halls and cozy lounge exude old Florentine charm
$$ Hotel Axial Via de' Calzaiuoli 11 | tel. 055-218-984 www.hotelaxial.it	Businesslike hotel two floors below its sister Hotel Maxim, higher prices but only slightly nicer rooms
$$ B&B Dei Mori Via Dante Alighieri 12 | tel. 055-211-438 www.deimoriit	5 colorful rooms on quiet lane, convivial living room, helpful staff, no elevator
$$ Hotel Alessandra Borgo S.S. Apostoli 17 | tel. 055-283-438 www.hotelalessandra.com	Tranquil and sprawling, with 27 big, old-school rooms and tiny Arno-view terrace
NORTH OF THE DUOMO—Not quite so central or picturesque but cheaper, located either near Mercato Centrale or the Accademia	
$$$ Hotel Loggiato dei Serviti Piazza S.S. Annunziata 3 tel. 055-289-592 www.loggiatodeiservitihotel.it	Former monastery near Accademia, Old World romance plus modern hair dryers, overflow annex
$$$ Hotel dei Macchiaioli Via Cavour 21 | tel. 055-213-154 www.hoteldeimacchiaioli.com	Fresh and spacious rooms in restored family-run palazzo, frescoed ceilings and modern comfort
$$ Residenza dei Pucci Via dei Pucci 9 | tel. 055-281-886 www.residenzadeipucci.com	13 pleasant, unique rooms spread over 3 floors (no elevator); soothing, rich decor gives this hotel an upscale ambience for its price range
$$ Hotel Morandi alla Crocetta Via Laura 50 | tel. 055-234-4747 www.hotelmorandi.it	Former convent on quiet street, period furnishings take you back centuries and up the social ladder
$$ Hotel Europa Via Cavour 14 | tel. 055-239-6715 www.webhoteleuropa.com	Cheery and family-run, spacious breakfast room, most rooms have Duomo views
$$ Relais Grand Tour Via Santa Reparata 21 | tel. 055-283-955 www.florencegrandtour.com	Cozy, artfully appointed B&B makes you feel right at home, spacious suites come with garden ambience, breakfast at corner bar, cash only

$$ Galileo Hotel Via Nazionale 22a | tel. 055-496-645 www.galileohotel.it	Comfortable business hotel, well-run with familial warmth, busy street but quiet rooms
$$ Hotel Il Bargellino Via Guelfa 87 | tel. 055-238-2658 www.ilbargellino.com	Summery residential ambience, antique furniture and modern paintings, momentum-slowing terrace, no breakfast
$ Casa Rabatti Via San Zanobi 48 black tel. 055-212-393	Practice your Italian with owner Marcella, the ultimate warm Italian mama; 4 simple, clean rooms; no air-con, no breakfast, cash only, overflow annex
$ Hotel Enza Via San Zanobi 45 black tel. 055-490-990 www.hotelenza.it	Predictable comfort in 18 straightforward rooms, some recently renovated, no elevator

EAST OF THE DUOMO—Good value conveniently tucked away in an untouristed, unassuming area a few blocks behind the church

$$ Residenza il Villino Via della Pergola 53 | tel. 055-200-1116 www.ilvillino.it	Quiet refuge with 10 charming rooms and picturesque, peaceful little courtyard
$$ Panella's Residence Via della Pergola 42 | tel. 055-234-7202 www.panellaresidence.com	Classy B&B in former convent, with 5 chic, romantic, and ample rooms; antique furnishings
$ Locanda de' Ciompi Via Pietrapiana 28 | tel. 055-263-8034 www.bbflorencefirenze.com	5 tidy and affordable rooms, overlooks Piazza dei Ciompi antique market, young and lively neighborhood
$ Hotel Dalí Via dell'Oriuolo 17 | tel. 055-234-0706 www.hoteldali.com	Cheap, cheery rooms, nice location, charming idealistic owners; no air-con, breakfast, or elevator
$ Oblate Sisters of the Assumption Borgo Pinti 15 | tel. 055-248-0582 sroblateborgopinti@virgilio.it	Convent-run old building, dreamy garden and public spaces, simple rooms w/single beds, prayerful ambience, cash only, 23:30 curfew

WEST OF THE DUOMO—Efficient location between train station and tourist action, mostly clustered near lively San Lorenzo church

$$$ Hotel Centrale Via dei Conti 3 | tel. 055-215-761 www.hotelcentralefirenze.it	Midway between station and Duomo, 31 spacious (though overpriced) rooms, tasteful mix of old and new
$$ Bellevue House Via della Scala 21 | tel. 055-260-8932 www.bellevuehouse.it	Oasis of tranquility; 6 spacious, old-fashioned rooms; no breakfast or elevator
$$ Hotel Accademia Via Faenza 7 | tel. 055-293-451 www.hotelaccademiafirenze.com	21 old-school rooms and a floor plan that defies logic; overpriced but conveniently located
$ Hotel Lorena Via Faenza 1 | tel. 055-282-785 www.hotellorena.co	Youth-hostel feel, some rooms with bathroom down hall, flexible rates, family-run with care

SOUTH OF THE ARNO RIVER (OLTRARNO)—Farther from the tourists, but nearer to crafts shops, neighborly piazzas, and family eateries

$$$ Hotel Silla Via dei Renai 5 | tel. 055-234-2888 www.hotelsilla.it	Classic three-star comfort; 36 cheery, spacious rooms; breezy terrace, faces the river
$$$ Hotel la Scaletta Via de' Guicciardini 13 | tel. 055-283-028 www.hotellascaletta.it	36 bright, remodeled rooms; rooftop terrace overlooking Boboli Gardens; tortured floor plan
$ Istituto Gould Via dei Serragli 49 | tel. 055-212-576 www.istitutogould.it	Church-run former palace w/ garden courtyard; 40 clean, spartan twin rooms; modern facilities, pay extra for air-con
$ Soggiorno Alessandra Via Borgo San Frediano 6 tel. 055-290-424 www.soggiornoalessandra.it	5 bright, small yet comfy rooms; double-paned windows cut noise, basic breakfast in room, air-con extra
$ Casa Santo Nome di Gesù Piazza del Carmine 21 | tel. 055-213-856 www.fmmfirenze.it	Convent in big old palace, 25 simple rooms w/twin beds, tranquil garden, no air-con, smiling nuns, 1:00 curfew
$ Ostello Santa Monaca (Youth Hostel) Via Santa Monaca 6 | tel. 055-268-338 www.ostellosantamonaca.com	Big well-run clean-enough institution attracts young backpackers, 114 beds in 13 rooms

Sleeping

Eating

Florentines are masters of the art of fine eating. Located in the heart of the Tuscan breadbasket, Florence enjoys some of the world's great rustic cuisine. Lingering over a multicourse meal with loved ones while you sip wine from nearby villages...it's one of Florence's great pleasures.

I list a full range of restaurants and eateries—from budget options for a quick bite to multicourse splurges with maximum ambience. I prefer mom-and-pop, personality-driven places, offering fine value and high quality with a local clientele.

When in Florence, I eat on the Florentine schedule. For breakfast, I eat at the hotel or grab a pastry and cappuccino at the neighborhood bar. Lunch is fast and simple to make time for sightseeing—a small sandwich (like many locals), a self-service cafeteria, or a picnic on a piazza bench.

Restaurant Price Rankings

> **$$$** Most main courses €15 or more.
> **$$** Most main courses €10-15.
> **$** Most main courses €10 or less.
>
> Based on the average price of a meat or seafood dish (a *secondo*) on the menu. Pastas, salads, and appetizers are a couple of euros cheaper. So a typical meal in a $$ restaurant—including appetizer, main dish, house wine, water, and service—would cost about €30. Circled numbers in the restaurant listings indicate locations on the maps on ✪ pages 154-157.

Dinner is the time for slowing down and savoring a restaurant meal. And then there's gelato...

Restaurants

Restaurants serve lunch from 13:00 to 15:00 (and rarely open their doors before noon). Dinner is served to Florentines after 21:00 and to tourists at 19:00 (quality restaurants rarely open any earlier).

Get used to the reality that many restaurants (even my recommendations) are frequented by fellow tourists—it's inevitable in crowded Florence. Minimize the tourist hordes by eating later, enjoying local ambience at lunchtime (when restaurants cater to office workers), or by escaping to the less-touristed Oltrarno area.

A full restaurant meal comes in courses: appetizer (antipasto), plate of pasta, meat or seafood course *(secondo),* salad, dessert, coffee, liqueurs, and so on. It can take hours, and the costs can add up quickly, so plan your strategy before sitting down to a restaurant meal.

For light eaters, there's nothing wrong with ordering a single dish as your meal—a plate of pasta, a pizza, an antipasto, or a salad. Couples could each order a dish (or two) and share. If you want a full meal at a predictable price, consider the *menu turistico*—a fixed-price multicourse meal where you can choose from a list of menu items. It includes the service charge, and is usually a good value for non-gourmets.

In Florence, only rude waiters rush you. For speedier service, be prepared with your next request whenever a waiter happens to grace your table. You'll have to ask for the bill—mime-scribble on your raised palm or ask: *"Il conto?"* Check your bill carefully for additional (dishonest) charges.

Quick Budget Meals

Florence offers many budget options for hungry travelers.

Italian "bars" are cafés, not taverns. These neighborhood hangouts serve coffee, sandwiches (grilled *panini* or cold *tramezzini*), mini-pizzas, pre-made salads, fresh squeezed orange juice *(spremuta),* and drinks from the cooler.

Various cafeteria-style places (called *tavola calda, rosticceria,* or "self-service cafeterias") dish out fast and cheap cooked meals to eat there or take out. You can buy pizza by the slice at little hole-in-the-wall places, sold by weight (100 grams for a small slice). Ethnic joints serve Turkish *döner kebabs* (meat and veggies wrapped in pita bread) and falafel (a fried garbanzo-bean patty). A wine bar *(enoteca)* sells wine by the glass, but they also serve meat-and-cheese-type plates for the business crowd at lunch and happy hour.

At any eating establishment (however humble), be aware that the price of your food and drink may be 20-40 percent more if you consume it while sitting at a table instead of standing at the bar. This two-tier price system will always be clearly posted. Don't sit without first checking out the financial consequences. Also, at many bars, the custom is to first pay the cashier for what you want, then hand the receipt to a barista who serves you.

Picnicking saves euros and time, lets you sample regional specialties, and puts you in contact with everyday Florentines in the marketplace. Buy a sandwich or slice of pizza "to go" *(da portar via),* get fruit at the corner grocery store *(supermercato),* pick up a bottle of wine, refill your water bottle at a public tap...and dine like a Medici amid atmospheric surroundings. Florence's large covered farmers market, the Mercato Centrale (✪ see page 120), is a picnic-shopper's paradise. When buying produce, it's customary to let the merchant pick it out. If something is a mystery, ask for a small taste—*"Un assaggio, per favore?"*

Florentine Cuisine

Along with the basic dishes you'll find all over Italy, Florence has its signature specialties. Florentine cuisine is hearty, simple farmers' food: grilled

Gelato

The Florentines claim they invented gelato, or Italian-style ice cream. Many think it's the world's best. Gelato uses slightly less milk fat than American-style ice cream, letting the natural flavors come through. It's generally homemade on the premises, proudly advertised as *artiginale, nostra produzione,* or *produzione propia.*

Check the price board listing the different size cups and cones. Choose your container (for example, "a €3 cone" or "a €4 cup"), then point out the flavors you want. They'll let you put more than one flavor in even the smallest container.

Try free samples before ordering—*"Un assaggio, per favore?"* (A taste, please?). Ask the server what flavors go well together—*"Che si sposano bene?"* (What "marries" well?). Afficionados avoid the bright, chemical-colored flavors that draw children. Don't limit your tasting to a single *gelateria.* When it comes to gelato in Florence, I say, *Perchè no?*—Why not?

meats, high-quality vegetables in season, fresh herbs, prized olive oil, beans, and rustic bread.

For appetizers, try *panzanella,* a summery tomato salad with bread chunks, or pecorino cheese, made from ewe's milk. *Ribollita* is a bean soup. A classic main dish is *bistecca alla fiorentina,* a steak grilled very rare (and sold expensively by the gram—confirm the total price). Florentines love fresh game, such as boar *(cinghiale)* or game birds. *Spiedino* is roast meats on a skewer. Anything described as *"...alla fiorentina"* (in the Florentine style) usually means it's cooked with vegetables, especially spinach. Florentines traditionally eat lots of tripe *(trippa)*—intestines—as good as it sounds.

No meal in Italy is complete without wine. Even the basic house wine *(vino da tavola* or *vino della casa)* is fine with a meal. Tuscany is world-renowned for producing hearty Sangiovese-grape reds that pair well with meat dishes. The famous Chianti wine is grown 20 miles south of Florence. More complex (and expensive) is Brunello di Montalcino, or its cheaper cousin, Rosso di Montalcino. Vino Nobile di Montepulciano is a dry ruby red that's much better than the "Montepulciano" wine sold in US grocery stores. The so-called "Super Tuscans" are a creative new breed of wines made from non-native grapes now grown in Italy. For a crisp white, try Orvieto Classico.

Italian coffee is some of the world's best. Even the most basic hole-in-the-wall bar serves quality espresso, *macchiatos,* and cappuccinos. In summer, Florentines like a sugared iced coffee called *caffè freddo.*

Popular liqueurs to finish a meal are *amaro* (various brands) and anise-flavored Sambuca. Florentines love dipping biscotti in *vin santo* (literally "holy wine"), a sweet, golden dessert wine. Or pick up a cup or cone of gelato at a *gelateria* and stroll the streets with the rest of Florence, enjoying a bit of edible art.

THE DUOMO TO THE ARNO RIVER—Historic, atmospheric, overpriced, and touristy—better to just grab a quick lunch while sightseeing	
❶ $ Self-Service Ristorante Leonardo Via Pecori 11 tel. 055-284-446	Inexpensive, air-conditioned, quick, a block SW of Baptistery, hardworking staff, free water (daily 11:45-14:45 & 18:45-21:45)
❷ $$$ Frescobaldi Ristorante and Wine Bar Via dei Magazzini 2 red tel. 055-284-724	Aristocratic, formal, candlelit ambience and great wine, dress-up dinners, more casual lunch (daily 12:00-14:30 & 19:00-22:30)
❸ $ Cantinetta dei Verrazzano Via dei Tavolini 18 tel. 055-268-590	Sandwich plates and wine in old-time setting, light meals for office workers, delicious cakes (Mon-Sat 8:00-21:00, Sun 10:00-16:30)
❹ $ Osteria Vini e Vecchi Sapori Via dei Magazzini 3 red tel. 055-293-045	Colorful hole-in-the-wall restaurant serving Tuscan food, fun and accessible, reserve for dinner (Mon-Sat 12:30-14:30 & 19:30-22:30, closed Sun)
❺ $ I Fratellini Via dei Cimatori tel. 055-239-6096	Informal, longstanding sandwich-and-wine eatery, order something exotic, sit on curb with locals (daily 9:00-19:30 or until the bread runs out)
❻ $ Il Cernacchino Via della Condotta 38 red tel. 055-294-119	Handy, well-regarded shop selling *panino* sandwiches (Mon-Sat 9:30-19:30, closed Sun)

Eating

NORTH OF THE DUOMO—Better value than the historic center, but still many fellow tourists. Find these near the Mercato Centrale or the Accademia.

❼	**$$ Trattoria Zà-Zà** Piazza del Mercato Centrale 26 red tel. 055-215-411	Fun, high-energy place serves Tuscan specialties to happy tourists, arrive early or make reservation, check bill carefully (daily 11:00-23:00)
❼	**$ Trattoria Mario's** Via Rosina 2 tel. 055-218-550	Lunch-only local fixture, bustling service, home cooking, good value, shared tables, arrive early, cash only (Mon-Sat 12:00-15:30, closed Sun and Aug)
❽	**$$ Trattoria la Burrasca** Via Panicale 6 tel. 055-215-827	Small friendly Flintstone-chic eatery, good-value seasonal home cooking, popular with my readers (Tue-Sun 12:00-15:00 & 19:00-22:30, closed Mon)
❾	**$$ Pepò** Via Rosina 4 red tel. 055-283-259	Colorful, charmingly unpretentious neighborhood eatery serving simple yet well-prepared Florentine classics (daily 12:00-14:30 & 19:00-22:30)
❿	**$-$$ Mercato Centrale (Central Market)** Just north of the Basilica of San Lorenzo	Upstairs: gleaming foodie mecca with a dozen upscale food counters and restaurants (daily 10:00-24:00). Ground floor: market zone filled with raw ingredients, picnic delicacies, and humble food counters (Mon-Fri 7:00-14:00, Sat 7:00-17:00, closed Sun)
❿	**$ Nerbone in the Market** Inside Mercato Centrale mobile 339-648-0251	Inside the Mercato Centrale, venerable diner for cheap sit-down meal with fellow shoppers, cash only (lunch menu served Mon-Sat 12:00-14:00, sandwiches from 8:00 until the bread runs out, closed Sun)
⓫	**$ Casa del Vino** Via dell'Ariento 16 red tel. 055-215-609	Well-regarded wine shop serves small sandwiches to mobs of locals on lunch break (Mon-Sat 9:30-20:30 year-round, closed Sun year-round, Sat in summer, and Aug)

⑫	**$ Pasticceria Robiglio** Via dei Servi 112 red tel. 055-212-784	Near the Accademia, elegant little café, limited menu but generous spirit (daily 12:00-15:00, longer hours as a café)
⑬	**$ La Mescita Fiaschetteria** Via degli Alfani 70 red mobile 347-795-1604 or 338-992-2640	Untouristed student-filled hole-in-the-wall; pasta, sandwiches, cheap wine; point to what you want, check your bill (Mon-Sat 11:30-15:30, closed Sun)
⑭	**$ Carrefour Express** Via Ricasoli 109 red	Handy supermarket with sandwich counter and picnic supplies, eat on historic Piazza S.S. Annunziata (Daily 8:00-20:00)

EAST OF THE DUOMO—Find these between the Palazzo Vecchio and Santa Croce Church

⑮	**$ Ristorante del Fagioli** Corso dei Tintori 47 tel. 055-244-285	Proud, enthusiastic family serves loyal customers home-style classics, reserve for dinner, cash only (Mon-Fri 12:30-14:30 & 19:30-22:30, closed Sat-Sun)
⑯	**$ All'Antico Vinaio** Via dei Neri 65 red tel. 055-238-2723	Florentine favorite, offers stand-up wining and sandwich dining, sit-down place across the street (Mon-Sat 12:00-23:00, Sun 12:00-16:00)
⑰	**$ Trattoria Anita** Corner of Via Vinegia and Via del Parlagio at #2 red tel. 055-218-698	Wood paneling and rows of wine bottles, three-course weekday lunch specials (Mon-Sat 12:00-14:30 & 19:00-22:15, closed Sun)
⑱	**$$ Trattoria l'cche C'è C'è** Via Magalotti 11 red tel. 055-216-589	EE-kay chay chay; "whatever there is, there is"), small mom-and-pop place, tourist-filled but fun, Florentine dishes (Tue-Sun 12:30-14:30 & 19:30-22:30, closed Mon and two weeks in Aug)

WEST OF THE DUOMO—Near the church of Santa Maria Novella

⑲	**$$ Trattoria al Trebbio** Via delle Belle Donne 47 tel. 055-287-089	Traditional food (rabbit, steak), simple candlelit elegance inside or outside on romantic square (daily 12:00-15:00 & 19:00-23:00)

⑳	**$$ Trattoria "da Giorgio"** Via Palazzuolo 100 red tel. 055-284-302	Family-style home cooking makes a fun night out for happy locals and tourists, fixed-price meal a great value (Mon-Sat 12:00-14:30 & 18:00-22:00, closed Sun)
㉑	**$$ Trattoria Marione** Via della Spada 27 red tel. 055-214-756	Sincerely cooked home-style meals in crowded, happy atmosphere beneath hanging ham hocks (daily 12:00-17:00 & 19:00-23:00)
㉒	**$$ Trattoria Sostanza-Troia** Via del Porcellana 25 red tel. 055-212-691	Famous for (splittable) steaks and pastas, crowded, shared tables, reserve for dinner, cash only (open Mon-Sat, dinner seatings at 19:30 and 21:00, closed Sun year-round and Sat off-season)
㉓	**$$ Panini Tartufati Procacci** Via Tornabuoni 64 red tel. 055-211-656	Swanky wine bar specializes in truffle-scented ingredients; reasonably priced sandwiches, pricey sampler plates (Mon-Sat 10:00-20:00, closed Sun)
SOUTH OF THE ARNO RIVER (OLTRARNO)—More out-of-the-way but more authentic. Florentines may even outnumber my readers.		
㉔	**$$$ Golden View Open Bar** Via dei Bardi 58 tel. 055-214-502	Ponte Vecchio view; noisy, touristy bistro for salad, pizza, or pasta with fine wine; reserve for window, jazz lounge drinks (19:00-21:30) include free appetizers (daily 11:30-24:00)
㉕	**$$ Il Santo Bevitore Ristorante** Via di Santo Spirito 64 red tel. 055-211-264	Dark and dressy tables, creative Tuscan cuisine paired with wine, come early or reserve, casual wine bar next door (daily 12:30-14:30 & 19:30-22:30, closed Sun for lunch)
㉖	**$$ Trattoria 4 Leoni** Piazza della Passera (between Ponte Vecchio and Piazza di Santo Spirito) tel. 055-218-562	Quintessential Oltrarno scene on colorful square, traditional but creative food, good house wine, reservations wise (daily 12:00-24:00)
㉗	**$$ Antico Ristoro Di' Cambi** Via Sant'Onofrio 1 red tel. 055-217-134	Meat lover's dream, rustic bustling beer-hall energy, confirm full price of your sold-by-weight *bistecca* (Mon-Sat 12:00-14:30 & 18:30-22:30, closed Sun)

㉗	**$ Trattoria Sabatino** Via Pisana 2 red tel. 055-225-955	Untouristed, spacious, brightly lit mess hall; little English, simple menu, disturbingly cheap (Mon-Fri 12:00-14:30 & 19:15-22:00, closed Sat-Sun)
㉗	**$$$ Trattoria da Sergio** Borgo San Frediano 145 red tel. 055-223-449	Tiny and charming, gourmet home-cooking, loyal customers make reservations a must (Tue-Sat 12:00-14:00 & 19:30-22:45, Sun 12:00-14:00, closed Mon)
㉘	**$$$ Olio & Convivium** Via di Santo Spirito 4 tel. 055-265-8198	Romantic and a little formal, for well-dressed foodies, good-value sampler plates, wines by the glass, air-con (Tue-Sun 12:00-14:30 & 19:00-22:30, closed Mon)
㉙	**$$ Trattoria Al Tranvai** Piazza Torquato Tasso 14 red tel. 055-225-197	Locals cram into dark-wood tables, like a small town's favorite eatery (Mon 19:00-24:00, Tue-Sat 12:30-14:30 & 19:30-22:30, closed Sun)
㉚	**$ Trattoria Casalinga** Via de' Michelozzi 9 red tel. 055-218-624	Aproned women bustle serving hordes of Florentines and happy tourists, near colorful Santo Spirito (Mon-Sat 12:00-14:30 & 19:00-22:00, closed Sun and Aug)
㉛	**$$ Caffè Ricchi** Piazza di Santo Spirito 8 red tel. 055-215-864	Nice Santo Spirito setting, fine pasta, gelato, homemade desserts (daily 7:00-24:00, until 21:00 in winter)

Eating

Florence Restaurants

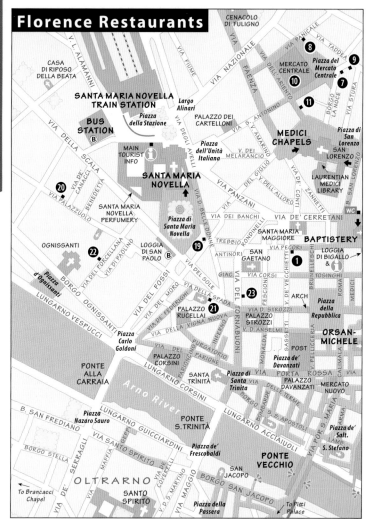

CENACOLO
DI FULIGNO

V. L. ALAMANNI

VIA PANIGALE

VIA TADDEA

8

CASA
DI RIPOSO
DELLA BEATA

VIA NAZIONALE

VIA FIUME

VIA FAENZA

VIA DELL'ARIENTO

MERCATO
CENTRALE

10

*Piazza del
Mercato
Centrale*

9

7

**SANTA MARIA NOVELLA
TRAIN STATION**

*Largo
Alinari*

BORGO
LA NOCE

VIA STURA

BUS
STATION
B

*Piazza
della Stazione*

PALAZZO DEI
CARTELLONI

V. S. ANTONINO

11

*Piazza di
San
Lorenzo*

VIA DELLA SCALA

MAIN
TOURIST
INFO **i**

*Piazza
dell'Unità
Italiana*

V. DEI
MELARANCIO

**MEDICI
CHAPELS**

SAN
LORENZO

V. S. N. BENEDETTA

VIA DE' CANACCI

**SANTA MARIA
NOVELLA**

VIA DE' CONTI

VIA DE' GINORI

LAURENTIAN
MEDICI
LIBRARY

20

VIA PALAZZUOLO

SANTA MARIA
NOVELLA
PERFUMERY

VIA DEL GIGLIO

VIA PANZANI

VIA D. BELLE DONNE

VIA DEI BANCHI

VIA DE' CERRETANI

WC

SANTA MARIA
MAGGIORE

VIA PECORI

BAPTISTERY

OGNISSANTI

22

VIA DEL PORCELLANA

VIA DI PAOLINO

LOGGIA
DI SAN
PAOLO **B**

*Piazza di
Santa Maria
Novella*

19

TREBBIO RONDINELLI

ANTINORI

SAN
GAETANO

VIA DE' VECCHIETTI

VIA DE' PESCIONI

VIA BRUNELLESCHI

LOGGIA
DI BIGALLO
& **i**

TOSINGHI

*Piazza
d'Ognissanti*

BORGO OGNISSANTI

VIA DEL SOLE

VIA DEL MORO

VIA DELLA SPADA

VIA DE' FOSSI

GIAC.

VIA DEI CORSI

23

VIA STROZZI

PALAZZO
STROZZI

V. D. ANSELMI

SASSETTI

ROMA

MEDICI

LUNGARNO VESPUCCI

PALAZZO
RUCELLAI

21

VIA DELLA VIGNA NUOVA

VIA DE' FEDERIGHI

VIA DE' TORNABUONI

POST

*Piazza
della
Repubblica*

**ORSAN-
MICHELE**

*Piazza
Carlo
Goldoni*

PALAZZO
CORSINI

VIA DEL PARIONE

VIA DEL FIORDALISO

INFERNO

PURGATORIO

*Piazza de'
Davanzati*

V. PELLICCERIA

CALIMALA

VIA PORTA ROSSA

VIA

**PONTE
ALLA
CARRAIA**

LUNGARNO CORSINI

SANTA
TRINITÀ

*Piazza di
Santa
Trinita*

VIA PORTA ROSSA

PALAZZO
DAVANZATI

MERCATO
NUOVO

Arno River

B. SAN FREDIANO

*Piazza
Nazaro Sauro*

LUNGARNO GUICCIARDINI

PONTE
S.TRINITÀ

BORGO SS. APOSTOLI

LUNGARNO ACCIAIUOLI

VIA POR S. MARIA

*Piazza de'
Salt.*

S. Stefano

VIA DE' SERRAGLI

VIA MAFFIA

VIA SANTO SPIRITO

VIA DE' COVERELLI

*Piazza de'
Frescobaldi*

**PONTE
VECCHIO**

BORGO STELLA

OLTRARNO

VIA DE' GEPPI

V. DE' MICHELOZZI

SAN
JACOPO

BORGO SAN JACOPO

→ To Brancacci
Chapel

**SANTO
SPIRITO**

VIA S. AGOSTINO

VIA MAGGIO

*Piazza della
Passera*

→ To Pitti
Palace

Eating

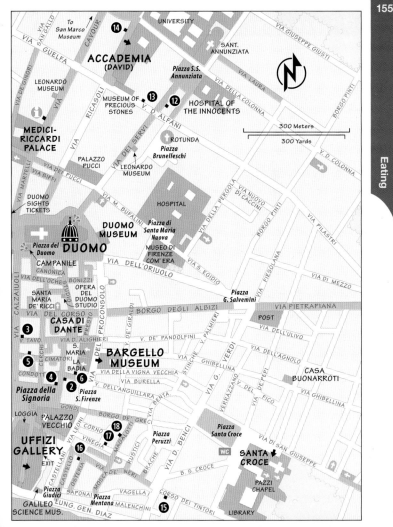

Oltrarno Restaurants

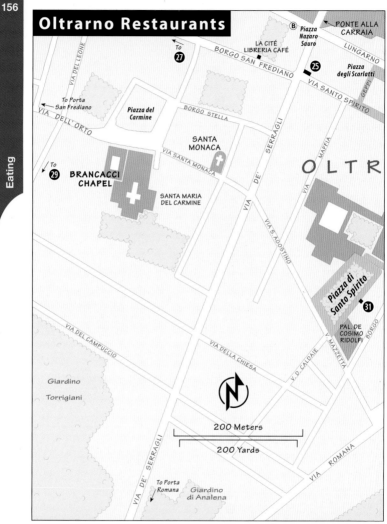

Eating

PONTE ALLA CARRAIA

B Piazza Nazaro Sauro

LA CITÉ LIBRERIA CAFÉ

BORGO SAN FREDIANO

LUNGARNO

25

Piazza degli Scarlatti

VIA DEL LEONE

To 27

VIA SANTO SPIRITO

GEPPI

To Porta San Frediano

Piazza del Carmine

BORGO STELLA

VIA DELL'ORTO

SANTA MONICA

VIA SANTA MONICA

VIA DE SERRAGLI

VIA MAFFIA

O L T R

To 29

BRANCACCI CHAPEL

SANTA MARIA DEL CARMINE

VIA S. AGOSTINO

Piazza di Santo Spirito

31

BORGO

VIA DEL CAMPUCCIO

VIA DELLA CHIESA

V. MAZZETTA

PAL. DE COSIMO RIDOLFI

V.D. CALDAIE

Giardino Torrigiani

N

200 Meters

200 Yards

VIA DE' SERRAGLI

VIA ROMANA

To Porta Romana

Giardino di Analena

VIA ROMANA

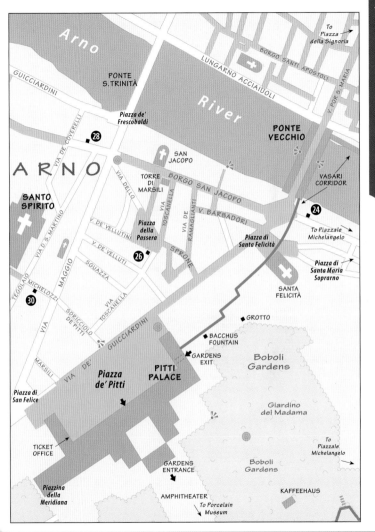

Practicalities

PLANNING

When to Go

Tuscany's best travel months (also its busiest and most expensive) are April, May, June, September, and October. These months combine the convenience of peak season with pleasant weather. July and August sizzle with temperatures into the 90s (get a hotel with air-conditioning). November to March (with temperatures in the 40s and 50s) have none of the sweat and stress of the tourist season, but sights may have shorter hours. Even off-season, Florence can be crowded on holiday weekends. Any time of year, many sights are closed on Monday and close early on Sunday.

Before You Go

Make sure your passport is up to date (to renew, see www.travel.state. gov). Call your debit- and credit-card companies about your plans (see below). Book hotel rooms in advance, especially for travel during peak season or holiday weekends. Consider buying travel insurance (see www. ricksteves.com/insurance). If traveling beyond Florence, research transit schedules (trains, buses) and car rentals. If renting a car, you're technically required to have an International Driving Permit (sold at your local AAA office), though I've often rented cars in Italy without one. Consider making reservations for key sights (✪ see page 170). Get a current list of museum hours at www.firenzeturismo.it.

MONEY

Italy uses the euro currency: 1 euro (€) = about $1.10. To convert prices in euros to dollars, add about 10 percent: €20 = about $22, €50 = about $55. (Check www.oanda.com for the latest exchange rates.)

Withdraw money from a cash machine using a debit card, just like at home. Visa and MasterCard are commonly used throughout Europe. Before departing, call your bank and credit-card company: Confirm that your card will work overseas, ask about international transaction fees, and alert them that you'll be making withdrawals in Europe. Many travelers bring a second debit/credit card as a backup. Cash is always good to have on hand, so withdraw large amounts (€250-300) from the ATM.

American credit cards—even new ones with a chip—may not work

Helpful Websites

Italian Tourist Information: www.italia.it
Florence Tourist Information: www.firenzeturismo.it
Cheap Flights: www.kayak.com (for international flights), www.skyscanner.com (for flights within Europe)
European Train Schedules: www.bahn.com
General Travel Tips: www.ricksteves.com (trip planning, packing lists, and more—plus updates for this book)

in some payment machines (e.g., ticket kiosks) geared for European-style chip-and-PIN cards. Be prepared to pay with cash, try entering your card's PIN, or find a nearby cashier.

To keep your valuables safe, wear a money belt. But if you do lose your credit or debit card, report the loss immediately with a phone call: Visa (tel. 303/967-1096), MasterCard (tel. 636/722-7111), and American Express (tel. 623/492-8427).

ARRIVAL IN FLORENCE

Amerigo Vespucci Airport (a.k.a. Peretola)
Florence's airport is about five miles northwest of the city. Though small, it has all the services you'd expect—a TI, ATMs, car-rental agencies, cafés, and shops (airport code: FLR, no overnighting allowed, airport info tel. 055-306-1830, flight info tel. 055-306-1300—domestic only, www.aeroporto.firenze.it).

To get between the airport and downtown, you have two main options:

Taxi: Expect to pay about €25 for the 30-minute ride.

Budget Shuttle Buses: These connect the airport (departing from the far right as you exit the arrivals hall) with Florence's train and bus stations (described later; from the bus station, it's a 20-minute walk to the Duomo, or take a city bus or taxi). Airport shuttle buses depart twice an hour daily 5:00-23:30, and take 30 minutes (€6—buy your ticket on board).

Returning to the airport from Florence, the first bus leaves the bus station at 5:30.

Santa Maria Novella Train Station

Florence's main train station (called Firenze S.M.N. to distinguish it from Florence's two smaller stations) is on the western edge of the historic center, an easy 10- to 15-minute walk to the Duomo.

With your back to the tracks, get oriented. To the left is baggage storage (halfway down track 16). Directly ahead—outside the station—is a TI, located straight across the square, 100 yards away. To the right (also outside the station) is the handy Sapori & Dintorni Conad supermarket, for sandwiches and salads to go. Avoid long ticket-window lines by using the easy-to-master ticket machines, or use a travel agency near your hotel.

To get into town, exit the station to the left. There you'll find taxis (€8 to the Duomo) and city buses (buy tickets at the ATAF ticket office inside the main station hall). To walk into town (10-15 minutes), exit the station through the main hall and head straight across the square outside (toward the Church of Santa Maria Novella). On the far side of the square, keep left and head down the main Via dei Panzani, which leads directly to the Duomo.

BusItalia Bus Station

Located 100 yards west of the Florence S.M.N. train station on Via Santa Caterina da Siena, this is the hub for regional buses to Siena, San Gimignano, and other Tuscan hill towns, plus the shuttle bus to and from Florence's Amerigo Vespucci Airport. For most buses, buy tickets in the station, or pay 30 percent more if you pay on board. Bus service drops dramatically on Sunday. Bus info: Tel. 800-373-760 or www.fsbusitalia.it.

To walk into town (20 minutes to the Duomo), exit the station through the main door, and turn left along the busy street toward the brick dome. The train station is on your left, while downtown Florence is straight ahead and a bit to the right.

Tips for Drivers

Don't drive into the Florence city center. Strictly enforced laws ticket those without a permit to enter the *Zona Traffico Limitato.* Instead, park your car at one of several big parking lots on the perimeter, where you can catch a bus or taxi into the center. Find a lot *("trova parcheggio")* at www.firenze parcheggi.it.

Arrival by Cruise Ship at the Port of Livorno

The coastal town of Livorno is about 60 miles west of Florence. A day-trip into Florence is doable but busy, involving at least two hours of round-trip travel. To do it on your own by bus-and-train is, frankly, too much trouble. The easiest option is to book an excursion through your cruise line. Or, hire a private taxi or minibus—these are waiting at the dock as travelers disembark. They'll drive you into Florence (one-hour trip), give you about five hours of sightseeing time, then bring you back to the port. Establish a total price beforehand and pay at the end.

HELPFUL HINTS

Tourist Information (TI): At any TI, pick up a current listing of museum hours. This is very important, because hours can change from month to month (or download the current list at www.firenzeturismo.it). TIs also have city maps, but many hotels do, too. The TIs at the train station and on Via Cavour sell the Firenze Card (✪ see page 169).

The main TI sits 100 yards directly across the square from the **train station,** but it's very crowded (Piazza della Stazione 4, Mon-Sat 9:00-19:00, Sun 9:00-14:00, tel. 055-212-245, www.firenzeturismo.it). Another branch is right by the **Duomo** (on Piazza del Duomo inside the Loggia, Mon-Sat 9:00-19:00, Sun 9:00-14:00). A third TI is a block-and-a-half **north of the Duomo** (Via Cavour 1 red, Mon-Fri 9:00-18:00, closed Sat-Sun, tel. 055-290-832).

Hurdling the Language Barrier: Most people in the tourist indus-try—and virtually all young people—speak at least a little English. Still, learn the pleasantries such as *buon giorno* (good day), *mi scusi* (pardon me), *per favore* (please), *grazie* (thank you), and *arrivederci* (goodbye). For more Italian survival phrases, ✪ see page 177.

Time Zones: Italy is generally six/nine hours ahead of the East/West coasts of the US.

Business Hours: Most businesses are open throughout the day Monday through Saturday, generally 9:00-19:00, and closed Sunday. But hours can vary widely from store to store. Some small businesses close for lunch (roughly 13:00-15:30). Banking hours are generally Monday through Friday 8:30 to 13:30 and 15:30 to 16:30. Some stores are closed on Monday, and they may close earlier on Saturday. Many Florence shops close for a couple of weeks around August 15.

Watt's Up? Europe's electrical system is 220 volts, instead of North America's 110 volts. You'll need an adapter plug with two round prongs, sold inexpensively at travel stores in the US. Most newer electronics (such as mobile devices, laptops, hair dryers, and battery chargers) convert automatically, so you won't need a separate converter.

Numbers and Stumblers: What Americans call the second floor of a building is the first floor in Europe. Europeans write dates as day/month/year, so Christmas is 25/12/16. Commas are decimal points and vice versa—a dollar and a half is 1,50, and there are 5.280 feet in a mile.

Italy uses the metric system: A kilogram is 2.2 pounds; a liter is about a quart; and a kilometer is six-tenths of a mile. Temperature is measured in Celsius. 0°C = 32°F. To roughly convert Celsius to Fahrenheit, double the number and add 30.

Holidays: Many sights and banks close down on national holidays. Verify dates at www.italia.it or www.firenzeturismo.it, or check www.rick steves.com/festivals.

Addresses: Florence has a ridiculously confusing system for street addresses. They use "red" numbers (e.g., Via Cavour 52r) for businesses, and "black" numbers (e.g., Via Cavour 25n) for residences. I'm lazy and don't concern myself with the distinction—if one number's wrong, I look nearby for the other.

Internet Access: Nearly all Florence hotels have Wi-Fi free for guests, and many cafés and restaurants will share their network password if you buy something. The city has a free Wi-Fi hotspot network that covers all the main squares in town (no registration, good for two hours). For an Internet café with public computers, ask your hotelier or check the touristy area near San Lorenzo Market and the train station (especially along Via Faenza).

Bookstores: You can pick up cheap, pretty-good art-and-history guidebooks at kiosks and museums. For English guidebooks (including mine), try Paperback Exchange (south of the Duomo at Via delle Oche 4 red) or RED (on Piazza della Repubblica).

Laundry: The Wash & Dry Lavarapido chain has self-service launderettes at several locations: Via dei Servi 105 red (near *David*), Via della Scala 52 red (near train station), Via Ghibellina 143 red (Palazzo Vecchio),

Tipping

Tipping in Europe isn't as automatic and generous as it is in the US. At Italian restaurants that have waitstaff, a "service" charge (*servizio*) of about 10 percent is usually included in your bill's grand total. Italians don't tip beyond this, but if the service is exceptional, you can round up the bill by a euro or two. At hotels, it's polite to give porters a euro for each bag (another reason to pack light). To tip a taxi driver, round up to the nearest euro (for a €5.50 fare, give €6), or up to 10 percent for longer rides.

and Via dei Serragli 87 red (Oltrarno). Most are open daily 8:00-22:00 (about €8 for wash and dry, bring plenty of coins, tel. 055-580-480).

Free Water: Carry a water bottle to refill at twist-the-handle public fountains, like the one to the left of the Palazzo Vecchio.

Services: WCs are scarce. Use them when you can, in any café or museum you patronize.

Be Ready: Though small, Florence is intense. Prepare for scorching summer heat, slick pickpockets, few WCs, steep prices, and long lines. Easy tourist money has corrupted some locals, making them greedy and dishonest (check your bill carefully).

GETTING AROUND FLORENCE

Because Florence is so compact, I walk everywhere. I mainly use buses to reach outlying sights (Piazzale Michelangelo or Fiesole) and taxis to shuttle me and my bags between the hotel and the train station/airport.

On Foot: I think of Florence as my Renaissance treadmill—after three days of walking, I have the buns of *David*. Much of the historic core is pedestrian-only, but it's still an intense urban environment of narrow streets, tourist crowds, and busy locals speeding through on bicycles and motorbikes.

Buses: A single ticket is €1.20, good for 90 minutes. A 24-hour pass is €5. Buy tickets at tobacco shops (*tabacchi*), newsstands, the ATAF ticket window inside the train station, or on board for a bit more (€2, exact change). Validate your ticket in the machine on board. Most buses leave from two major hubs: the train station or Piazza San Marco (near the Accademia). For bus information, get a transit map at the ATAF ticket window, call 800-424-500, or check www.ataf.net.

I find these to be most helpful bus lines:

#C2 twists through the congested old center from the train station to the Santa Croce neighborhood. Just €1.20 gets you a 90-minute joyride.

#C1 stops near the Palazzo Vecchio and Piazza Santa Croce, then heads north to Piazza Libertà.

#D goes from the train station to Ponte Vecchio, then cruises through Oltrarno as far east as Ponte San Niccolò.

#12 goes from the train station to the Oltrarno, Piazzale Michelangelo, and San Miniato Church. Bus #13 makes the return trip down the hill.

#7 goes from Piazza San Marco (near the Accademia) to Fiesole (small town with views).

Taxi: The minimum cost is €5 (€8.30 after 22:00, or €7 on Sun). Taxi fares and supplements are clearly explained on signs in each taxi—rides in the center of town should be charged as tariff #1. A typical taxi ride from the train station to the Duomo costs about €8; from Ponte Vecchio to Piazzale Michelangelo costs about €10. It can be hard to hail a cab on the street. To call one (€2 extra), dial 055-4390 or 055-4242.

Bike Rental: The city of Florence rents bikes cheaply (€2/1 hour, €10/day) at the train station, Piazza Santa Croce, and Piazza Ghiberti (east of the Duomo). Get info at a TI or mobile 346-883-7821.

STAYING CONNECTED

The easiest (if not cheapest) way to stay connected while on the road—planning your sightseeing, contacting hotels, and staying in touch back home—is to bring your own mobile device (phone, smartphone, tablet, or laptop) and keep your home carrier. But you can also do fine bringing no device at all, relying only on your hotel's computer, Internet cafés, and public phones. Read on for more details and budget alternatives. For more on all of these options, see www.ricksteves.com/phoning.

Using the Internet: Traveling with a mobile device gives you on-the-go access to the Internet and travel-oriented apps. You can make free or cheap phone calls using Skype, Google+ Hangouts, or Facetime.

To avoid sky-high fees for data roaming, disable data roaming entirely, and only go online when you have Wi-Fi (e.g., at your hotel or in a café). Or you could sign up for an international data plan for the duration of your trip: $30 typically buys about 100 megabytes—enough to view 100 websites or send/receive 1,000 emails.

Most hotels offer some form of free or cheap Internet access—either a shared computer in the lobby or Wi-Fi in the room. Otherwise, your hotelier can point you to the nearest Internet café. You'll also find Wi-Fi hotspots at many cafés (Wi-Fi is sometimes called "WLAN" in Italy).

Making Phone Calls: Many US mobile phones work in Europe. Expect to pay around $1.50 a minute for phone calls and 50 cents per text message (less if you sign up for an international calling plan with your service provider). If you plan to make a lot of calls, consider outfitting your phone with a European SIM card—that is, temporarily sign up with a European carrier. (For more on how SIM cards work, see www.ricksteves.com/phoning).

It's easy to buy a phone in Europe, which costs more up front but is cheaper by the call. You'll find mobile-phone stores selling cheap phones (as little as $40) and SIM cards at the airport and train station, and throughout Florence.

Dialing Tips: Always start with the **international access code**—011 if you're calling from the US or Canada, 00 from anywhere in Europe. If you're dialing from a mobile phone, simply insert a + instead (by holding the 0 key.) To call **from the US to Italy,** dial 011 (US access code), 39 (Italy's country code), 0, and the local number. To call from **any European country to the US,** dial 00 (Europe's access code), 1 (US country code), then the area code and local number. **To call within Italy,** just dial the number (Italy does not use area codes). If you're calling other European countries whose phone numbers begin with 0, you'll usually have to omit that 0 when you dial. If you're calling from Europe using your US mobile phone, dial as if you're calling from the US.

Phoning Inexpensively: Here's a budget alternative if you don't carry a mobile phone: Buy an international phone card (€5). This gives you pennies-per-minute rates on international calls, decent rates for calls within Italy, and can even be used from your hotel phone or a European mobile phone. Buy cards at newsstands, *tabacchi* (tobacco) shops, train stations, and post offices. Tell the vendor where you'll be making the most calls (*"per Stati Uniti"*—to America), and he'll select the most economical brand.

Practicalities

Useful Contacts

English-Speaking Police Help: Tel. 113
Ambulance: Tel. 118
Directory Assistance: Tel. 170 (free, in English) or tel. 12 (€0.50, in Italian)
US Embassy (in Rome): 24-hour emergency line—tel. 06-46741, non-emergency—tel. 06-4674-2420, (by appointment only, Via Vittorio Veneto 121, Rome, http://italy.usembassy.gov)
US Consulate (in Florence): Tel. 055-266-951, http://florence.us consulate.gov
Canadian Embassy (in Rome): Tel. 06-854-442-911, www.italy.gc.ca

Calling from your hotel room without a phone card can be a rip-off—ask your hotelier about their rates before you dial.

SIGHTSEEING TIPS

Plan Ahead to Avoid Crowds: Avoid long ticket-buying lines at major sights by making reservations, buying a Firenze Card, or buying combo-tickets (these options are described in more detail later in this section). This is especially necessary from April through October and on all holiday weekends.

Hours: Check opening hours carefully and plan your time well. Some sights have erratic hours (e.g., closed the second and fourth Monday of the month). Hours can change season-to-season, so get the most up-to-date list from a TI or at www.firenzeturismo.it. Many sights are closed Monday and have shorter hours Sunday. Many sights stop admitting people 30-60 minutes before closing time, and guards start shooing people out, so don't save the best for last.

What to Expect: Important sights have metal detectors or conduct bag searches that will slow your entry. Some don't allow large bags or don't allow you to bring liquids (water bottles) in. Photos and videos are normally allowed, but flashes or tripods usually are not.

Dress Code at Churches: Some sights are also churches, and they may enforce a modest dress code—no shorts, bare shoulders, or mini-skirts. You'll find this at the Duomo, Santa Maria Novella, Santa Croce, and the Medici Chapels. Some churches sell cheap, disposable ponchos for instant respectability. Other churches encourage a dress code but don't enforce it. Churches that aren't major sights usually close from around 12:30 to 15:30.

Discounts: Many sights offer discounts for seniors, families, and students or teachers with proper identification cards (www.isic.org). Always ask. Children under 18 sometimes get in for free or cheap. Some discounts are only for EU citizens.

Pace Yourself: Schedule cool breaks into your sightseeing where you can sit and refresh with a drink or snack.

Rick Steves' Free Audio Tours: I've produced free, self-guided audio tours of the Renaissance Walk, the Accademia/*David,* and the Uffizi Gallery. Download them via the Rick Steves Audio Europe smartphone app, www.ricksteves.com/audioeurope, iTunes, or Google Play.

Firenze Card

The Firenze Card (€72) is pricey but convenient. This three-day sightseeing pass gives you admission to many of Florence's sights, including the Uffizi Gallery, the Accademia, and the Duomo-related sights. Just as important, it lets you skip the ticket-buying lines without making reservations. For busy sightseers, the card can save some money. And for anyone, it can certainly save time.

With the card, you simply go to the entrance at a covered sight (if there's a "with reservations" door, use it), show the card, and they let you in.

Add up your sightseeing to see if it's worth it: Uffizi Gallery (as much as €16.50 with temporary exhibits plus reservation fee) + Accademia (€16.50) + Bargello (€11) + Medici Chapels (€12) + Palazzo Vecchio (€14), and so on. Factor in the time saved waiting in ticket lines, and the freedom to pop into lesser sights you otherwise wouldn't pay for. If you're planning to see five or six major sights in a short time, the card pays for itself.

You can buy the card at many participating museums. The least-crowded outlet is the TI a couple of blocks north of the Duomo at Via Cavour 1 red. To get the most from your card, validate it only when you're ready to tackle the covered sights in 72 consecutive hours (e.g., 15:00 Tue until 15:00 Fri). Note that not all of Florence's sights are covered. For a complete list of included sights, see www.firenzecard.it.

Advance Reservations

If you decide not to get a Firenze Card, you can avoid ticket lines by making reservations (€4 per ticket booking fee) at key sights. I recommend them for the Uffizi Gallery (book weeks or months in advance) and the Accademia (a few days ahead is usually enough). Off-season (Nov-March), reservations may not be necessary if you visit in late afternoon on weekdays, and are willing to endure some waiting time. There are several ways to make a reservation:

• **Through Your Hotel:** When you make your hotel reservation, ask if they can book your museum reservations, too.

• **By Phone:** From the US, dial (011-39)-055-294-883 to reach an English-speaking operator who walks you through the process in a few minutes. Lines are open Mon-Fri 8:30-18:30, Sat 8:30-12:30 (Italian time). The line is often busy, so be persistent.

• **Online:** Using a credit card, you can book through the city's official site, www.firenzemusei.it (€4/ticket fee). More user-friendly are booking sites www.uffizi.com or www.tickitaly.com, but their fees are steep—about €10 per ticket.

• **Reserve in Florence:** If you arrive without a reservation, try the booking window at Orsanmichele Church (daily 9:00-16:00, closed Sun off-season) or the My Accademia Libreria bookstore across from the Accademia (Tue-Sun 8:15-17:30).

Note that reservations are not possible on the first Sunday of the month, when the museums are free.

Combo-Ticket for the Duomo and Related Sights

Five Duomo-related sights are covered by a €15 combo-ticket (no individual tickets): the Duomo's dome, Campanile, Baptistery, Duomo Museum, and Santa Reparata crypt (inside the Duomo). (Admission to the Duomo itself is free.) You can buy tickets at the office opposite the Baptistery entrance; at the Campanile, Santa Reparata crypt, and Duomo Museum (lines at the museum are usually the shortest). Tickets are not sold at the dome. Even with a Firenze Card, to visit the Duomo sights, you'll need to get a free ticket at the ticket office opposite the Baptistery.

THEFT AND EMERGENCIES

Theft

While violent crime is rare in the city center, thieves (mainly pickpockets) thrive in crowds. Be alert to the possibility of theft, even when you're absorbed in the wonder and newness of Florence. Be on guard whenever crowds press together, while you're preoccupied at ticket windows, anywhere around major sights, and while boarding and leaving buses. Be especially alert around Florence's train station, the station's underpass (and where the tunnel surfaces), near Santa Maria Novella and Santo Spirito, and on the popular bus #7 to Fiesole. Assume that any beggar or friendly petitioner is really a pickpocket, and any commotion in the crowd is a distraction by a team of thieves.

I keep my valuables—passport, credit cards, crucial documents, and large amounts of cash—in a money belt that I tuck under my beltline. Dial 113 for English-speaking police help. To replace a passport, contact an embassy or consulate (for contact info, ✪ see page 168). File a police report without delay; it's required to submit an insurance claim for lost or stolen rail passes or travel gear, and can help with replacing your passport or credit and debit cards. For more information, see www.ricksteves.com/help.

Medical Help

Dial 113 for English-speaking police/medical emergencies, or 118 for an ambulance. If you get sick, do as the Italians do and go to a pharmacy, where qualified technicians routinely diagnose and prescribe. Or ask at your hotel for help—they'll know the nearest medical and emergency services. English-speaking doctors include Medical Service Firenze (tel. 055-475-411) or Dr. Stephen Kerr (tel. 055-288-055, mobile 335-836-1682, www.dr-kerr.com).

ACTIVITIES

Shopping

Florence is a great shopping town, known for its sense of style since Medici days. It offers the full range, from glitzy high-fashion boutiques to haggle-till-you-drop street markets. Many smaller stores use *siesta* hours—open

Monday to Saturday 9:00-13:00 and 15:30-19:30, closed Sunday, and often closed on Monday.

High-Fashion Boutiques: The entire area **between the Duomo and the Arno River** bristles with trendy fashion boutiques. The Gucci Museum (€7), right on Piazza della Signoria, tells the story of that famous designer. The Ponte Vecchio houses gold and silver shops. The upscale La Rinascente department store is on Piazza della Repubblica.

Via de' Tornabuoni, three blocks west of Piazza della Repubblica, is especially classy, home to the Ferragamo handbag-and-shoe store (Via de' Tornabuoni 2) and its nearby shoe museum (Piazza Santa Trinità 5). Also nearby, check out Via Strozzi, Via della Vigna Nuova, and Via del Parione.

Markets: Every day, the **San Lorenzo Street Market** (✪ see page 120) offers stalls of touristy goods (leather bags, T-shirts, trinkets) in the streets ringing the large covered market known as the **Mercato Centrale.** Inside the Mercato Centrale is an upscale food court and food and produce vendors (✪ see page 120). **Mercato Nuovo** (three blocks north of Ponte Vecchio) is an open-air loggia with souvenir items (✪ see page 113). In the **Santa Croce area** (southeast of the Duomo), the Piazza dei Ciompi flea market runs daily, but only really hops on the last Sunday of the month. The area hosts several bargain leather stores and the pricey leather school inside Santa Croce Church (✪ see page 122). South of the river in the **Oltrarno,** find antiques and artisan shops on and around Via Toscanella.

Souvenir Ideas: You won't need a guidebook to find all kinds of art-themed posters, calendars, Botticelli mouse pads, Raphael lipstick-holders, and plaster *David*s. With its history as a literary center, Florence offers traditional marbled stationery, leather-bound journals, fine pens, and reproductions of old manuscripts. Tuscan hand-painted ceramics are popular. Italian foods—olives, cheese, pesto—must conform to US Customs rules (see below). Bringing fragile bottles of Italian wine home in your luggage is legal but can be a recipe for disaster.

Sizes: European clothing sizes are different from the US. For example, a woman's size 10 dress (US) is a European size 40, and a size 8 shoe (US) is a European size 38-39.

Getting a VAT Refund: If you spend more than €155 on goods at a single store, you may be eligible to get a refund of the 22 percent Value-Added Tax (VAT). You'll need to ask the merchant to fill out the necessary refund document, then process your refund through a service such as

Global Blue or Premier Tax Free, with offices at major airports. For more details, see www.ricksteves.com/vat.

Customs for American Shoppers: You are allowed to take home $800 worth of items per person duty-free, once every 31 days. You can also bring in duty-free a liter of alcohol. As for food, you can take home many processed and packaged foods (e.g., vacuum-packed cheeses, chocolate, mustard). Fresh produce and most meats are not allowed. Any liquid-containing foods must be packed (carefully) in checked luggage. To check customs rules and duty rates, visit http://help.cbp.gov.

If You Go Overboard: To bring all of your booty home, you can buy a cheapo suitcase (for as little as €25) at the stalls outside the Church of Santa Maria Novella, opposite the train station.

Entertainment and Nightlife

For me, nighttime is for eating a late meal, catching a concert, strolling through the old town with a gelato, or hitting one of the many pubs. Find English-language films at the Odeon Cinema (near Piazza della Repubblica on the Piazza Strozzi, tel. 055-214-068, www.odeonfirenze.com). Get the latest on nightlife and concerts from *The Florentine* magazine (free from the TI) or *Firenze Spettacolo* (bought from newsstands), or check www.firenzespettacolo.it or www.firenzeturismo.it.

Stroll from the Duomo to the Arno: Join the parade of locals on their evening *passegiata,* strolling the pedestrian zone, enjoying cafés, *gelaterias,* great people-watching, and street performers. Pop into a wine bar *(enoteca)* to sample regional wines by the glass or a plate of meats and cheeses. (Psst. Near the Duomo, find La Congrega Lounge Bar—a tiny retreat on a tiny lane just off the main pedestrian drag, at Via Tosinghi 3/4 red.) End at the Arno, to stand atop Ponte Vecchio and watch the sun set, the moon rise, and lovers kiss. Other great nighttime scenes are the viewpoints at Piazzale Michelangelo (✪ page 133) and Fiesole (✪ page 133).

Live Music: Orsanmichele Church, in the heart of Florence's historic core, hosts chamber music under its Gothic arches. Tickets are sold on the day of the concert from the door facing Via de' Calzaiuoli. Santo Stefano Church, near Ponte Vecchio, hosts concerts almost nightly (on Piazza San Stefano, tel. 055-289-367, www.notearmoniche.com). Orchestra della Toscana, near the Bargello, presents major classical concerts from November to May (Via Ghibellina 97 red, tel. 055-212-320, www.orchestra dellatoscana.it). St. Mark's English Church, south of the Arno, offers opera (Via Maggio 18, mobile 340-811-9192, www.concertoclassico.info). Golden View Open Bar, a river-view restaurant near Ponte Vecchio, has live jazz three nights a week at 21:00 (✪ see page 152). The Box Office sells tickets for rock concerts and more (Via delle Vecchie Carceri 1, tel. 055-210-804, www.boxofficetoscana.it).

Late-Night Partying: With so many American and international college students in town, Florence by night can have a frat-party atmosphere. Piazza Santa Croce and bars along nearby Via de' Benci are the epicenter of international-student partying, with occasional rock concerts in the square. For a more local crowd, head south from Santa Croce across the river (crossing Ponte alle Grazie) to find a few late-night bars at Piazza Demidoff. In the Oltrarno southwest of Ponte Vecchio, Piazza di Santo Spirito is trendy and bohemian but also seedy.

Guided Tours

Hop-On Hop-Off Bus Tours: Double-decker buses give tourists a drive-by look at major landmarks while they listen to recorded descriptions. But since many important sights are in the pedestrian-only historic core, Florence doesn't really lend itself to this kind of tour—check out the route map before committing (€20 for one calendar day, pay as you board, www.firenze.city-sightseeing.it).

Walking and Bicycle Tours: Many companies offer English-language, 2- to 3-hour small-group tours of Florence's sights, for around €25-75 a person. Some offer a Rick Steves discount—it's worth asking.

Artviva Walking Tours offers a variety of tours of the town, the main museums, day-trips, bike tours, and cooking classes (office is above Odeon Cinema near Piazza della Repubblica, tel. 055-264-5033, www.artviva.com). Florencetown Tours does walking tours, biking tours, and cooking classes (Via de Lamberti 1, tel. 055-281-103, www.florencetown.com). For a more scholarly approach, try Walks Inside Florence (mobile 335-526-6496, www.walksinsideflorence.com), Florentia (www.florentia.org), or Context Florence (tel. 06-967-27371, US tel. 800-691-6036, www.contexttravel.com).

If you'd like a private guide (around €70/hour), consider Alessandra Marchetti (mobile 347-386-9839, aleoberm@tin.it) or Paola Migliorini (tel. 055-472-448, mobile 347-657-2611, www.florencetour.com).

Cooking Classes, Art-Making, and More: Most of the tour companies listed above also offer Florence experiences. I've enjoyed cooking classes, a paint-your-own-fresco art class, food-oriented walks, Tuscan day trips, lectures, kids' programs, wine tours, and more. Check their websites.

RESOURCES FROM RICK STEVES

This Pocket guide is one of dozens of titles in my series of guidebooks on European travel. I also produce a public television series, *Rick Steves' Europe*, and a public radio show, *Travel with Rick Steves*. My website, www.ricksteves.com, offers a wealth of free travel resources, including videos and podcasts of my shows, audio tours of Europe's great sights, travel forums, guidebook updates, and information on European rail—plus an online travel store and specifics on our tours of Europe. If you want to be my virtual travel partner, follow me on Facebook and Twitter as I share my latest news and on-the-road spills, thrills, and insights. If you have feedback on this book, please fill out the survey at www.ricksteves.com/feedback. It helps us and fellow travelers.

Italian Survival Phrases

English	Italian	Pronunciation
Good day.	Buon giorno.	bwohn JOR-noh
Do you speak English?	Parla inglese?	PAR-lah een-GLAY-zay
Yes. / No.	Sì. / No.	see / noh
I (don't) understand.	(Non) capisco.	(nohn) kah-PEES-koh
Please.	Per favore.	pehr fah-VOH-ray
Thank you.	Grazie.	GRAHT-seeay
You're welcome.	Prego.	PRAY-go
I'm sorry.	Mi dispiace.	mee dee-speeAH-chay
Excuse me.	Mi scusi.	mee SKOO-zee
(No) problem.	(Non) c'è un problema.	(nohn) cheh oon proh-BLAY-mah
Good.	Va bene.	vah BEHN-ay
Goodbye.	Arrivederci.	ah-ree-vay-DEHR-chee
one / two	uno / due	OO-noh / DOO-ay
three / four	tre / quattro	tray / KWAH-troh
five / six	cinque / sei	CHEENG-kway / SEHee
seven / eight	sette / otto	SEHT-tay / OT-toh
nine / ten	nove / dieci	NOV-ay / deeAY-chee
How much is it?	Quanto costa?	KWAHN-toh KOS-tah
Write it?	Me lo scrive?	may loh SKREE-vay
Is it free?	È gratis?	eh GRAH-tees
Is it included?	È incluso?	eh een-KLOO-zoh
Where can I buy / find...?	Dove posso comprare / trovare...?	DOH-vay POS-soh kohm-PRAH-ray / troh-VAH-ray
I'd like / We'd like...	Vorrei / Vorremmo...	vor-REHee / vor-RAY-moh
...a room.	...una camera.	OO-nah KAH-meh-rah
...a ticket to ___.	...un biglietto per ___.	oon beel-YEHT-toh pehr
Is it possible?	È possibile?	eh poh-SEE-bee-lay
Where is...?	Dov'è...?	DOH-veh
...the train station	...la stazione	lah staht-seeOH-nay
...the bus station	...la stazione degli autobus	lah staht-seeOH-nay DAYL-yee OW-toh-boos
...tourist information	...informazioni per turisti	een-for-maht-seeOH-nee pehr too-REE-stee
...the toilet	...la toilette	lah twah-LEHT-tay
men	uomini, signori	WOH-mee-nee, seen-YOH-ree
women	donne, signore	DON-nay, seen-YOH-ray
left / right	sinistra / destra	see-NEE-strah / DEHS-trah
straight	sempre diritto	SEHM-pray dee-REE-toh
When do you open / close?	A che ora aprite / chiudete?	ah kay OH-rah ah-PREE-tay / keeoo-DAY-tay
At what time?	A che ora?	ah kay OH-rah
Just a moment.	Un momento.	oon moh-MAYN-toh
now / soon / later	adesso / presto / tardi	ah-DEHS-soh / PREHS-toh / TAR-dee
today / tomorrow	oggi / domani	OH-jee / doh-MAH-nee

In the Restaurant

I'd like...	Vorrei...	vor-REHee
We'd like...	Vorremmo...	vor-RAY-moh
...to reserve...	...prenotare...	pray-noh-TAH-ray
...a table for one / two.	...un tavolo per uno / due.	oon TAH-voh-loh pehr OO-noh / DOO-ay
Non-smoking.	Non fumare.	nohn foo-MAH-ray
Is this seat free?	È libero questo posto?	eh LEE-bay-roh KWEHS-toh POH-stoh
The menu (in English), please.	Il menù (in inglese), per favore.	eel may-NOO (een een-GLAY-zay) pehr fah-VOH-ray
service (not) included	servizio (non) incluso	sehr-VEET-seeoh (nohn) een-KLOO-zoh
cover charge	pane e coperto	PAH-nay ay koh-PEHR-toh
to go	da portar via	dah POR-tar VEE-ah
with / without	con / senza	kohn / SEHN-sah
and / or	e / o	ay / oh
menu (of the day)	menù (del giorno)	may-NOO (dayl JOR-noh)
specialty of the house	specialità della casa	spay-chah-lee-TAH DEHL-lah KAH-zah
first course (pasta, soup)	primo piatto	PREE-moh peeAH-toh
main course (meat, fish)	secondo piatto	say-KOHN-doh peeAH-toh
side dishes	contorni	kohn-TOR-nee
bread	pane	PAH-nay
cheese	formaggio	for-MAH-joh
sandwich	panino	pah-NEE-noh
soup	minestra, zuppa	mee-NEHS-trah, TSOO-pah
salad	insalata	een-sah-LAH-tah
dessert	dolci	DOHL-chee
tap water	acqua del rubinetto	AH-kwah dayl roo-bee-NAY-toh
mineral water	acqua minerale	AH-kwah mee-nay-RAH-lay
milk	latte	LAH-tay
(orange) juice	succo (d'arancia)	SOO-koh (dah-RAHN-chah)
coffee / tea	caffè / tè	kah-FEH / teh
wine	vino	VEE-noh
red / white	rosso / bianco	ROH-soh / beeAHN-koh
glass / bottle	bicchiere / bottiglia	bee-keeAY-ray / boh-TEEL-yah
beer	birra	BEE-rah
Cheers!	Cin cin!	cheen cheen
More. / Another.	Ancora un po.' / Un altro.	ahn-KOH-rah oon poh / oon AHL-troh
The same.	Lo stesso.	loh STEHS-soh
The bill, please.	Il conto, per favore.	eel KOHN-toh pehr fah-VOH-ray
tip	mancia	MAHN-chah
Delicious!	Delizioso!	day-leet-seeOH-zoh

For more user-friendly Italian phrases, check out *Rick Steves' Italian Phrase Book & Dictionary* or *Rick Steves' French, Italian, and German Phrase Book*.

INDEX

Index

Index

Start your trip at

Our website enhances this book and turns

Explore Europe

At ricksteves.com you can browse through thousands of articles, videos, photos and radio interviews, plus find a wealth of money-saving travel tips for planning your dream trip. And with our mobile-friendly website, you can easily access all this great travel information anywhere you go.

TV Shows

Preview the places you'll visit by watching entire half-hour episodes of Rick Steves' Europe (choose from all 100 shows) on-demand, for free.

Start your trip at

Our website enhances this book and turns

Explore Europe

At ricksteves.com you can browse through thousands of articles, videos, photos and radio interviews, plus find a wealth of money-saving travel tips for planning your dream trip. And with our mobile-friendly website, you can easily access all this great travel information anywhere you go.

TV Shows

Preview the places you'll visit by watching entire half-hour episodes of Rick Steves' Europe (choose from all 100 shows) on-demand, for free.

ricksteves.com

your travel dreams into affordable reality

Radio Interviews

Enjoy ready access to Rick's vast library of radio interviews covering  travel tips and cultural insights that relate specifically to your Europe travel plans.

Travel Forums

Learn, ask, share! Our online community of savvy travelers is a great resource for first-time travelers to Europe, as well as seasoned pros. You'll find forums on each country, plus travel tips and restaurant/hotel reviews. You can even ask one of our well-traveled staff to chime in with an opinion.

Travel News

Subscribe to our free Travel News e-newsletter, and get monthly updates from Rick on what's happening in Europe.

Audio Europe™

Rick's Free Travel App

Get your FREE Rick Steves Audio Europe™ app to enjoy…

- Dozens of self-guided tours of Europe's top museums, sights and historic walks
- Hundreds of tracks filled with cultural insights and sightseeing tips from Rick's radio interviews
- All organized into handy geographic playlists
- For Apple and Android

With Rick whispering in your ear, Europe gets even better.

Find out more at ricksteves.com

Pack Light and Right

Gear up for your next adventure at ricksteves.com

Light Luggage

Pack light and right with Rick Steves' affordable, custom-designed rolling carry-on bags, backpacks, day packs and shoulder bags.

Accessories

From packing cubes to moneybelts and beyond, Rick has personally selected the travel goodies that will help your trip go smoother.

Rick Steves has

Experience maximum Europe

Save time and energy

This guidebook is your independent-travel toolkit. But for all it delivers, it's still up to you to devote the time and energy it takes to manage the preparation and logistics that are essential for a happy trip. If that's a hassle, there's a solution.

Rick Steves Tours

A Rick Steves tour takes you to Europe's most interesting places with great guides and small groups

great tours, too!

with minimum stress

of 28 or less. We follow Rick's favorite itineraries, ride in comfy buses, stay in family-run hotels, and bring you intimately close to the Europe you've traveled so far to see. Most importantly, we take away the logistical headaches so you can focus on the fun.

Join the fun

This year we'll take 18,000 free-spirited travelers—nearly half of them repeat customers—along with us on 40 different itineraries, from Ireland to Italy to Istanbul. Is a Rick Steves tour the right fit for your travel dreams? Find out at ricksteves.com, where you can also get Rick's latest tour catalog and free Tour Experience DVD.

Europe is best experienced with happy travel partners. We hope you can join us.

See our itineraries at ricksteves.com

Rick Steves®

Nearly all Rick Steves guides are available as ebooks. Check with your favorite bookseller.
Rick Steves guidebooks are published by Avalon Travel, an imprint of Perseus Books, a Hachette Book Group company.